Destined
to
Achieve

Destined
to
Achieve

Wisdom Principles for Fulfilling Your Dream

Bernard O.A. Antwi

BOA PUBLISHERS
COVENTRY

DESTINED TO ACHIEVE
WISDOM PRINCIPLES FOR FULFILLING YOUR DREAM
by
BERNARD O.A. ANTWI

Copyright © 2012 by Bernard Owusu Afriyie Antwi

ISBN 978-0-9573850-0-9

First Edition September 2012

Price : £ 6.99

Publishers :

BOA PUBLISHERS
2 HEN LANE HOLBROOKS
COVENTRY CV6 4LB
www.boapublishers.com

Printed by :
DTF Books, UK

So is my word that goes out from my mouth: It will not return to me empty, but will accomplish what I desire and achieve the purpose for which I sent it.

Isaiah 55:11

CONTENTS

ACKNOWLEDGEMENT

I give all glory and honour to the Almighty God for given me the wisdom and grace to write this book. Every perfect gift comes from Him.

To all those who gave their support and contributed in no small way to fulfil the plan of God for my life, I say a big thank you. While it may not be possible for me to list everyone, I wish to acknowledge the following: My parents: Mr and Mrs Antwi Barnieh, may God richly bless you for nurturing me in the way of the Lord. Special thanks go to my pastor in the Lord, Pastor Richard Kojo Acquah, for your great support for my ministry.

Also my appreciation goes to Pastor Olumuyiwa Kolawole of Redeemed Christian Church of God who read the draft and supported me to reach this far. May God continue to bless you sir.

Also many thanks go to my leaders and mentors in Christ; Rev Foster Akotia, Pastor Evremond Kukatula, Pastor Yaw Adjem, Pastor Prince Osei-Gyamfi, Prophet Maxwell Offei, Rev Mark Abban and Pastor Kwesi Gambrah. To all members of House of Revival (Coventry), thank you all for your prayers and support.

To Mr Kwame Boakye Sarpong for spending much of his time proofreading and ensuring all necessary amendments had been made. I want to salute Mr Harjeet Singh Sev of D.T.F Publishers and distributors for taking on the task of publishing this book.

Also my gratitude goes to the following people; Mrs Gloria Appiah, Mrs Vida Offei, Gabriella Antwi, Owusu BKweku, David Roman and Mr. Spanish, without their encouragement, this book would not have been here.

GOD BLESS YOU!

FOREWORD

Every born-again child of God is destined to achieve greatness in life, but it is unfortunate that a lot of believers do not experience this. This is not because God is unable, but because we have neglected the principles and instructions of God.

In Genesis 26, when there was famine in the land where Isaac dwelt, He wanted to go to Egypt. In verse 2 the Lord appeared to Isaac and instructed him not to go to Egypt, but to remain in the land.

Isaac listened and obeyed the voice and instruction of God and in verse 12 it was recorded that Isaac sowed in that very same land of famine and reaped a hundredfold because the Lord blessed him. Isaac became great and went forward and flourished because he listened to and obeyed God.

Bro. Bernard has outlined some principles through the help of the Holy Spirit. As you read and apply these principles, you will achieve greatness in life and fulfil your destiny.

Olumuyiwa Kolawole
Senior Pastor,
Redeemed Christian Church of God -
Jubilee Christian Centre, Coventry.

INTRODUCTION

Joseph had a dream, and when he told it to his brothers, they hated him all the more. He said to them, "Listen to this dream I had: We were binding sheaves of grain out in the field when suddenly my sheaf rose and stood upright, while your sheaves gathered around mine and bowed down to it."
Genesis 37:5-7

WHAT IS A DREAM?

A dream is an image of what you aspire to become in a future planted into your spirit by God.

In 2010, whilst meditating on what to write for my second book, I had a vision from God. In that vision the spirit of the Lord spoke to me concerning Joseph's dream. I could not understand initially but I began to hear, "Do you know how Joseph fulfilled his dream?"

I also heard, "Do you know it was not so much of Joseph's dream that brought him success but more importantly passing all the tests God sent through?" The Spirit of God then laid down many things in my heart for me to record for generations to come.

God is the giver of dreams and He has deposited specific dreams in each person.

Life is a journey and every great story begins with a dream. What dream has God given you to accomplish in this world? Can you record any dream God has laid in your heart? Do you know your purpose in life?

Your God-given dream defines your purpose in life. There are many different kinds of dreams in this world; I am not talking about man made dreams but God-given dreams. I know God has placed big dreams in your spirit that may seem impossible to accomplish but God-given dreams can always be fulfilled.

I have come to realise that the greatest tragedy is to allow what God has deposited in you to die while you are still alive. The saddest person on earth is not the poorest man without a penny in his pocket but a man without a dream. A man without a dream is like a man who does not know his purpose in life. Such person has nothing to live for and nothing to die for. God has not created you to be an experiment.

God has placed valuable dreams in people's hearts but distractions and challenges of life have caused many people to stop pursuing their dreams. Some have put theirs on hold and some are thinking of pursuing it in the future. One of the exciting truths about the future, which you cannot afford to disregard, is that the future is now and it begins now. Do you want to fulfil a truly meaningful life? Then start now. Your tomorrow is influenced by every decision you make today.

The Bible is filled with great heroes who were God-given dreams. Anyone who wants to accomplish a God given purpose must ask the giver of life for direction. The Bible says, "if any of you lacks wisdom, you should ask God, who gives generously to all without finding fault, and it will be given to you.' (James 1:5)

Destined to Achieve will guide you to understand the wisdom principles that would light up you path to success. Focusing on the tried and tested principles of success, it drives you to discover who you are and goads you on in the pursuit of your God-given dream.

PRINCIPLE 1

YOU ARE THE PURPOSE OF GOD

In Genesis chapter 37-50, the Bible records an account of a young man called Joseph, whose life was full of God-given dreams.

Joseph knew God had prepared a wonderful future for him. Every human being is a tool in the hands of God and Joseph was no exception. How he was going to fulfil his dream was not his greatest concern, because he understood that he was the purpose of God. He also understood the plan of God concerning his life.

Do you know God has a plan for your life? Every God-given dream will lead to a purpose driven life.

> *"For I know the plans I have for you," declares the LORD, "plans to prosper you and not to harm you, plans to give you hope and a future.*
> Jeremiah 29:11

Many dreams have been abolished in the land of the living because the carrier fails to understand that God has a plan for him and he is the purpose of God. Greater percentages of people are those who are just living without knowing their purpose in life. Also large numbers of Christians are those who just attend churches but do not know their purpose in life. They are moved by the social aspects of the church rather than focusing on building their spiritual life. This is why so many destinies remain unfulfilled in the Kingdom of God. People who understand that they are the purpose of God move in a high spirit and act differently.

> *I know that you can do all things; no purpose of yours can be thwarted.*
> Job 42:2

Joseph recognised that he was the purpose of God and did not allow anything to hinder him. He knew that God would use him to affect many people from generations to generations. Knowing this truth motivated him to keep his head high despite all the adversities he encountered in life.

There are many common men who recognised they were the purpose of God and accomplished greater things which many people would consider as impossible tasks for God.

Joseph was described as a wise man. He guided this truth with his whole heart and he was unique and exceptional in everything he did.

The people who know they are the purpose of God are kingdom minded. Their primary factor is the kingdom business. They also understand that the Kingdom of God is filled with many substitutes on the bench who are always willing to take their place so they do not joke concerning their purpose for the kingdom. Joseph understood why God had called him.

I would like you to meditate on these questions:

- Do you know God?
- Do you have a relationship with God?
- Do you know you are the purpose of God?

- If YES "have you taken a step"? And if NO just pray and ask Him for direction.

Let us consider some of the features that describe people who recognised they were the purpose of God and how they lived a triumphant life.

1. THEY FOCUS ON BUILDING THEIR INNER SPIRIT.

God's word is a spirit and life. God spoke his word into Joseph's spirit and he knew for him to gain access to what God had placed within him, he has to walk in spirit and in truth (John 4:24).

People who know they are the purpose of God focus on building their Inner Spirit. In Job 32:8, the Bible states, but there is a 'spirit in man and the breath of the Almighty gives him understanding'.

I have come to the understanding that the spirit in man is what connects him to his creator. It is through your Inner Spirit a person comes to know his true identity as a child of God. Knowing who you are is not based on your ethnic origin, race or family background but found in God.

Joseph knew who he was and did not place higher value on material things. While people place much value on earthly possessions such as cars, beauty, promotions, power and jobs. However, these are all temporary and do not even bring lasting happiness. People who know they are the purpose of God are aware that true joy comes as a total submission and fulfilment of God's word. They overcome the appetite of their earthly desires and seek to feed their Inner Spirit regularly.

Joseph rejected the offer of Potiphar's wife because he realised that would lead him to a temporary happiness. He chose to suffer afflictions because he knew that building the Inner Spirit is the most vital part of his walk with God.

Regardless to what you do, your deepest and the most lasting joy and strength will derive from knowing that you are the purpose of God.

To achieve your divine purpose, seek to build your Inner Spirit in order to be rooted in God to stand against the schemes of the enemy.

2. THEY ARE FAITHFUL

Faithfulness is one of the characteristics of the fruit of the Holy Spirit. It is a single fruit but contains many various qualities. People who realised they are the purpose of God are faithful. A faithful person is trustworthy and reliable.

> *Most men will proclaim each his own goodness, but who can find a faithful man?*
>
> Proverbs 20:6

Faithfulness is one of the greatest key in the Kingdom of God but many struggles to walk with God faithfully.

It is important you ask yourself this big question - "Can God really trust and rely on me?"

Joseph was a young man who walked faithfully with God. He (God) trusted Joseph and knew that when tested he will not give in to fornication.

God also knew when he becomes a minister in Egypt; he could count on him for greater accountability and greater management. The Bible shows great men who walk faithfully with God. A great example is our father, Abraham. All Christians declare that they are the heir not the tail. Anyone who declares this represents a royal since we are all descendants of Abraham. My question to you as a reader is, do royals live like slaves. No, they speak, eat, walk and behave like royals.

Do our characters resemble our forefathers in the Bible?

Nearly every step of father Abraham's life demonstrated faithfulness to God. David also showed great faithfulness to God as a young man. David acknowledged and repented immediately when he was convicted of his sin against God. Many of us find it hard to repent when we sin against God because of pride. (Proverb 28:13).

People who recognise that they are the purpose of God are faithful towards the things of God.

3. THEY ARE OBEDIENT TO GOD

Obedience is the automatic key to receiving God's blessings. Every step of Joseph's life demonstrated obedience to God. People who realise they are the purpose of God are obedient, they do not follow the voice of man but God.

The greatest commandment in the Bible is to love God by obeying his statutes (Mathew 22:36-38). Every child of God can only proof his love to God by obeying his word. (John 14:15).

Obedience results in a strong intimacy between God and man. Obedience also brings submission to God. Choosing to obey God means that you will collide with human thinking and the world system, but you have to trust in God's word.

Abraham is a good example of obedience. He left his family as soon as God visited him. He departed without complaining. Obedience brought him to his divine promise.

TRUE BLESSING AND DIVINE PROSPERITY COMES AS A RESULT OF OUR TOTAL OBEDIENCE AND SUBMISSION TO GOD.

Many people make a good start but end bad because of disobedience. A good example is Saul. (1 Samuel 15:2-11). Saul was a king who was highly anointed of God, and who everyone looked up to, but lacked wisdom and began to make decisions for himself. He lost favour in the sight of God due to self-glorification.

Partial obedience is equals to zero obedience. It is better to obey than to partially obey.

Every dream God place in a man will materialise when he acts according to the will of God. Obedience will enable you to realise the supremacy of God in your life.

4. THEY ARE HUMBLE

Humility is a quality we all despise since it can bring a man down and make others feel more superior.

HUMILITY IS THE DEEP AWARENESS OF UNWORTHINESS NOT WORTHLESSNESS.

Humility is not centred on appearance. It transcends beyond the physical. There are many people who are humble before men but not God. It is a right attitude of searching for deeper understanding than what you have already attained.

People who realize they are the purpose of God are humble. They are not proud or arrogant. They try everything possible to live at peace. In circumstances where conflict could have arisen, they take responsibility and seem capable to resolve them (Genesis 13:1-13). They are peacemakers.

They are people who understand the power of forgiveness. Their love toward other people never cease regardless to how awful they have been hurt or betrayed.

Joseph had every opportunity to retaliate against his brothers instead he chose to humble himself. The Bible states, God resists the proud but gives grace to the humble (James 4:6). He understood his position as a leader was not by his own effort but through the grace of God and he regarded no sin in his heart.

One key attribute that helps them to live peaceable with

all men is that, they regard everyone special and place value on them (Philippians 2:3-4).

Learn to be humble before God so that you can achieve your divine purpose.

5. THEY ARE RISK TAKERS

Joseph was a risk taker. All the heroes of the Bible took risks at certain point in their lives. History also proves that all successful people took risks before achieving their goals in life. Joseph's life was a demonstration of risk taking.

TAKING RISK MAKES A MAN RESPONSIBLE FOR HIS OWN LIFE.

People who understand they are the purpose of God learn to take risks. Man should be willing to make mistakes, hold unpopular positions and never be afraid to face big challenges. Discovering new ideas and new environments come as a result of taking risks.

Joseph knew that avoiding fornication with his master's wife could end him in an unfamiliar path for false accusation but took the risk to go to prison and keep his integrity before God. When a man takes risks for his life, dreams and goals become inevitable.

Another risk taker was David. He was a teenager who was never trained to use weapons or fight on the battlefield. The promise concerning his kingship was established when he took the risk to face Goliath. Imagine yourself as David, would you have quit or face Goliath as an untrained young man to fight a giant?

I pray that may the Almighty God grant you the strength to overcome every mountain in your life in Jesus's name. The disciples of Jesus Christ also took risks with their lives to bring the gospel to be where it is today.

The very nature of life requires risk taking. Every child takes risk to learn how to walk but yet knows he can fall and hurt himself. Think of risks as possibilities but not as danger. Begin to align your thinking to enhance the unknown paths as you pursue your divine dreams and visions in life. Taking risks increases maturity, honesty and brings prodigious accomplishments.

6. THEY DO NOT LIVE BY RECOGNITION

There is nothing wrong with being recognize or been appreciated for something good you have done. However, people who know they are purpose of God do not put much priority on recognition.

They keep on doing what God has entrusted them to do whether they are appreciated or not. They do everything from their heart for God not for man (Ecclesiastes 9:10). They know that their reward is in heaven. Their motive for doing things is always to glorify God and to promote God's kingdom and depopulate Satan's kingdom.

People who know they are the purpose of God live exceptional life. They can recognize spiritual truth beyond external situations. Joseph understood the plan of God concerning his life and focused on God purpose. Abraham, Jacob, Jeremiah, Nehemiah, David, Peter, Paul and many more knew they were the purpose of God and they did not give up.

Recognize that you are the purpose of God and pursue your divine call. There is no greater joy than fulfilling your divine mandate.

PRINCIPLE 2

PEOPLE

People are important instruments in all areas of life. We all need people in our lives. Nobody can succeed in remoteness. For anyone to prosper in life, he or she does not need only spiritual strength but also human empowerment.

Your relationship and how you deal with people will determine whether you will accomplish your God-given dream or not. Many people have given up their dreams because they failed to understand how to deal with people.

Joseph needed to understand he would meet different kinds of people in his life and also know how to deal with all of them in order to reach his dream.

I have met many people who ask this question: "How can people become impediment to achieving my dream?"

Life is full of relationships that bring both happiness and sorrow. In order for us to understand and reach our dreams, we need to know how to relate to people who come into our lives, because they form part of our dreams. God uses people to serve as bridges to our dreams. Every person that God brings along in your life has a role to play.

They may encourage you and also support you, but when it comes to fulfilling your God given dream in life, the greatest part lies with you. It is also important to understand that people in your life can become a stumbling block to fulfilling your destiny.

Your dream will draw people closer to you but that closeness does not signify that they want you to succeed. You will be surprised to see that out of one hundred people; only five truly love you and want to see your dream come to pass.

Joseph was an ambitious young man whose life was full of dreams. Joseph's life story is filled with great dramas of the Bible, extending from the innermost misery to a greatest triumph.

The Bible states, "this is what the Lord says: "Stand at the crossroads and look; ask for the ancient paths, ask where the good way is, and walk in it, and you will find rest for your souls." But you said, 'we will not walk in it." (Jeremiah 6:16).

Every dream given by God will bring different people in your life, but it is your responsibility to understand the role each of these people will play.

Here are examples of some of the kinds of people you will meet:

1. DREAM HATERS

Every dreamer attracts dream haters. Joseph sharing his big dreams with his brothers brought envy and jealousy. Your excitement will cause others to hate you.

The moment you announce your dream and vision, you incite close family members and close friends and other people to hate you more. Joseph's brothers hated him because they believed Joseph was not capable of accomplishing such an impossible dream.

Joseph's family hated him and even sold him to be a slave in a foreign land. The spiritual understanding of a slave means to lose your identity and to be rendered powerless.

Joseph had a dream, and when he told it to his brothers, they hated him all the more.

Genesis 37:5

People will hate you because they do not see what you can see. The bigger picture you can imagine is what gives you the energy to pursue your dream. Joseph's brothers hated him but he did not allow their intimidation to stop him from pursuing his big dreams. Be self-conscious with dream haters and prevent your dream at all cost.

2. DREAM KILLERS

When you begin to pursue your dream, it will attract people who will always try to kill your dream. Dream killers are inactive viewers who will contribute nothing positive or negative to affect your dream.

Joseph's brothers had an illegitimately inspired plan to kill off Joseph and kill his dream.

But they saw him in the distance, and before he reached them, they plotted to kill him. Here comes that dreamer!" they said to each other.

Genesis 37:18-19

The devil always believes he can frustrate the plan of God concerning man. Nobody can steal or kill your dream if it is ordained by God. Herod tried everything in his power to kill Jesus at birth (Mathew 2:9) and Moses had to endure a similar fate during the time of his birth, when all male children had to be killed (Exodus 1:22).

In the book of Samuel, David was also hated by King Saul when he was anointed by Prophet Samuel to be the next king of Israel (1 Samuel 19:1-2).

No dream opposition will stand against your God-given dream. Despite all the opposition and conspiracy in Joseph's life, he succeeded. Do not allow the opposition to steal, to kill and to destroy your dream (John 10:10).

3. DREAM ACCUSERS

Joseph was accused of a crime that he did not commit. Have you ever been accused of something you have never done or thought about?

The lies of Potiphar's wife led to Joseph being thrown into prison. The accuser's job is to prevent you from achieving your dream by means of distraction. Dream accusers are so heartless that they would say or do everything just to get you into trouble. They have the capacity to create perfect lies.

> Then she told him this story: "That Hebrew slave you brought us came to me to make sport of me. But as soon as I screamed for help, he left his cloak beside me and ran out of the house. When his master heard the story his wife told him, saying, 'This is how your slave treated me,' he burned with anger. 20 Joseph's master took him and put him in prison, the place where the king's prisoners were confined."
>
> Genesis 39:17-20

The dream accusers will watch you carefully in every step you take to see whether you will succeed in life or not. To become a dreamer, you cannot allow the voices and false allegations of dream accusers to frustrate you and destroy your God given dream. Through all the challenges, young Joseph kept his dream in his heart and never stopped dreaming.

Sometimes when we encounter people who are difficult to handle or have situations that seem beyond our control, things can get uncomfortable. It is always important to discern who is in your life so that you do not share your dream with the wrong people.

Do not be humiliated by dream haters, dream stealers and all the dream accusers. You are destined to succeed so keep focusing on the crown of accomplishing your dream.

PRINCIPLE 3

OVERCOMING EXCUSES

Life is full of obstacles and problems which make it easy and convenient to give excuses. Many people have the ability to accomplish great things but they are stuck on the path to pursuing their dreams and visions due to excuses. Since the creation of the earth, mankind has been fond of giving excuses...

> The man said, "The woman you put here with me-she gave me some fruit from the tree, and I ate it."
>
> Genesis 3:12

Excuses have kept many people below the standard of their true potential and hinder many from entering into their destiny space. Excuses are a part of the nature of mankind but it is vital for us to know that we cannot fulfil our dream when excuses lie along our paths.

Steven Grayham's quote:

> "Excuses are the tools with which persons with no purpose in view build for themselves great monuments of nothing."

The life of Joseph is one of the most inspiring success stories and has transformed many people's lives. Joseph had many reasons to give excuses but did not allow excuses to be a hindrance to his destiny. Joseph had experienced several difficulties in his life, from hatred and abuse from his brothers, who also sold him as a slave, to false imprisoned because of the lies of his master's wife. Yet, Joseph did not allow any of these bad experiences to become an excuse to his divine purpose. Even though he had many reasons to doubt God's promises concerning his life, He did not allow excuses to wreck his dreams.

As one becomes fond of making excuses, they become a habit and this may lead to negative repercussions in life. Excuses have the power to dominate and keep you stagnant in life.

Refuse to live in the world the world of excuses.

Those who have the ability to fill the earth with new inventions are living in the world of excuses. Why do people make excuses in life? Is it because they are born with excuses or through inheritance?

There are examples of men in the Bible who gave excuses when God called them to fulfil their purposes, such as, Moses, Gideon, Jeremiah, Saul and many more.

I love the story of a great hero Moses. He was a man called by God to liberate the children of Israel from bondage in Egypt. He was born to be a great leader but this was the same man that gave excuses when God called him. There is no one in the Bible who gave more excuses than Moses!

The most amazing thing is that God has all the answers to all our excuses we give when He calls us and places His word in our spirit. There are many people who are born to be great leaders, doctors, counsellors, lawyers, ministers of God, presidents and many more but they have allowed excuses to shut the door to their destinies.

What excuses did Moses give when God called him which can help us relate to our lives today? Let us see the excuses Moses and other heroes gave and how they can serve as hindrances to us from achieving our dreams in purposes today.

Excuses of Moses:

Excuses come in different forms and sizes. The first excuse Moses gave when God called him at the burning bush was;

1 WHO AM I?

WHO AM I, here means that, God has called Moses to accomplish a great plan in life but he saw himself as not qualified for the task. Most people in life are giving the same excuse as Moses. Most often, we think we are the wrong people to fulfil the task God has placed in our hands.

Why did Moses think he was not qualified for the job?

i. HIS PAST MISTAKES

Moses killed an Egyptian man and fled from Egypt. This evil act kept haunting him and made him feel inadequate to work for God. He thought he had failed in the sight of God, and was not qualified for such task. Moses knew committing murder was wrong.

Our past pasts failures often draw us back and hold our power to move forward in life. Most of us bear the same mentality as Moses. We use our past mistakes to make excuses to why we cannot pursue what God has place in our spirit.

We spend far too much time and energy thinking about things that cannot be changed. It is impossible to succeed in life without overcoming your past. Pray for direction and strength to move forward to bigger things.

Change is the law of life and those who look only to the past or present are certain to miss the future.

John F. Kennedy

ii. NOT WELL TRAINED

Moses thought he was insufficiently trained to deliver what God has given him to Pharaoh. There are many who give the same excuse as Moses. He realised that he would stammer when God called him and he felt he couldn't handle the pressure of delivering every word to Pharaoh.

God will never give you an assignment that you are unable to complete. God knows our ability. Even if we cannot handle the task, He still has a way of bringing people into our life to assist us through to the end. God knows our weaknesses and we do not have to be trained first for God to use us. He is the porter and he can mould us better for us to suit the specific task He has placed within us.

iii. AGE

Moses was 80 years when God called him to be a leader. It is conventionally hard to believe that a person at this age can still fulfil his earthly purpose but I have realised that God given dreams to mankind, are always beyond human understanding and age.

Most people with great ideas, visions and big innovations, which could bring advancement to the world, are held back by excuses, such as, 'can I do it',, 'I am too old for such a task' and 'I am not mature enough.'.

In pursuance of your dream, age should not be an impediment. The young as well as the elderly are all capable of achieving their lifelong dreams.

Prophet Jeremiah is an example of a person used his

age as an excuse to turn away from what God has assigned him to do. If it takes age to gain wisdom, then Methuselah, the oldest man ever lived on earth would have been the wisest man in history (Genesis 5:27) Wisdom is not of age neither as greatness.

iv. SIZE OF THE TASK

Moses thought that to become a leader was something bigger than him. There are many of us today who think they are not qualified enough to achieve their dreams. We have allowed self-limiting attitude to overcome us.

Because somebody tells you it's impossible or no one has achieved that in your family, does not mean that you cannot achieve your dream in life. Stop looking at the size of your dream and start to see yourself as bigger than the dream God has given you.

V. BACKGROUND AND INFERIORITY

Achievement is not limited to only certain people within a confined environment. Your location or place of birth does not determine who you are going to become in future. In the book of Judges 6:12, Gideon used his background as an excuse to protect his weakness and Saul also gave the same excuse when God called him to lead his nation from oppressions from the hands of the enemy (1 Samuel 9:21).

God created us in His image and that is how He sees us. God does not see our potentials based upon the family we come from, our status or our position in life.

> *"We have more ability than will power, and it is often an excuse to ourselves that we imagine that things are impossible."*
>
> Francois de la Rochefoucauld

Vi. SEND SOMEONE ELSE

Because Moses did not want to go, he told God to send someone else. Most times greatness in life comes with more responsibilities. Moses knew to become a leader was a great task therefore by escaping the leadership duties said he was not the right person for the task God was assigning him.

Finally, God knew the heart of Moses and great abilities of all the other heroes despite all the excuses they gave. God did not want Moses to live with those excuses so he sent Aaron to him to support the work

He has given to him. God has a way of dealing with us to overcome excuses. God does not want us to waste all the great treasures he has placed within us. Sometimes, our inadequate and inferiority stops us from pursuing our divine purpose in life. Moses is now remembered as one of the greatest prophet and heroes of the Bible because of his great courage.

We are all born with greatness and within us resides the power to break every chain of excuses.

PRINCIPLE 4

HAVE A CLEAR VISION

Where there is no vision, the people perish: but he that keepeth the law, happy he is.
Proverb 29:18

Every successful person or leader sees beyond the invisible. Vision is the ability to envision new things invisible to others. Every success or achievement is about understanding and applying the right principle. All successful people required clear vision of what they wanted to achieve in life. A dream without a clear vision is not a well-defined dream. The efficacy of every dream depends on clarity of vision.

Clear vision causes a person to plan well for the future. Visionary people have a picture of what they want to accomplish in their mind. Understanding clearly your vision helps you to overcome complications that lie with your dream. Without knowing what you want to achieve in life, it is impossible to create an outstanding outcome and succeed.

WHAT SEPARATES A VISIONARY PERSON FROM AN ORDINARY PERSON IS THE ABILITY TO SEE BEYOND IMAGINATION AND REACHING OUT TO THEM.

Despite the limitations of Helen Keller, she is still recognized as one of the most inspired women of all time.She lost her sight and hearing at the age of two, after contracting a mysterious disease that meant she could not see, hear or speak. This is what she said when asked what is more miserable than not having sight. Her response was; **"The only thing worse than being blind is having sight but no vision."**

Vision is extremely important. It supplies power and direction that will impact your thinking and actions. It is vital to understand that your daily actions show your destination.

Knowing what you want in life is a great step that everyone needs to fulfil their God-given purpose. After all, how are you going to reach a destination without knowing where you want to go in the first place?

You need the right vision to know your direction and destination. A person without a clear vision of where he is going has no reason to even begin his journey.

You are more likely to arrive anywhere on the road but that does not signify your destination.

> *For the vision is yet for an appointed time, but at the end it shall speak, and not lie: though it tarry, wait for it; because it will surely come, it will not tarry.*
>
> Habakkuk 2:3

I believe strongly that Joseph was a man with a clear vision of what his dream entailed. He had a vision of what he wanted to accomplish. As a young man, he understood that God was calling him to a place of leadership, authority and impartation that would cause his brothers and great men to bow at his feet.

Knowing the right vision is very important but not enough. There are very important steps that need to be followed in order to arrive at the right destination. The first thing to do when you have the right vision is to:

1. WRITE THE VISION

Your vision is not clear enough until you write it down. It has been said many times that, the world has room for people who show what they are capable of doing. Joseph, through insight, helped King Pharaoh by preparing and making provisions for the future to secure the famine on the land of Egypt for seven years.

Your vision must be clearly written so that it energizes many generations to follow it. It will also help you to keep track of what is ahead and saves you more time. Writing the vision gives you a clear picture and idea of what you are pursuing.

2. DEFINE THE VISION

Everyone is unique so is the vision you are carrying. It is vital that, people sit down and have enough time to plan and prepare. It is important you define and have full understanding of what your vision entails.

UNTIL YOU ARE ABLE TO DEFINE AND UNDERSTAND YOUR VISION, YOUR DREAM CANNOT MATERIALISE.

Knowing precisely what your vision entails will help you to avoid imitating other people but instead assist you to create your own unique path to fulfil your dream. Your vision becomes the primacy of your life when it is well defined and simplified.

3. RUN WITH THE VISION

The Bible says, 'faith without action is dead'. So is a vision without action (James 2:14-16).

To write and define your vision without running with it, is like having a great idea in your head but doing nothing and believing that you will just make it. You have to value the vision God has deposited within you.

Your vision should be big enough to make people think it is impossible to reach. Sometimes it may not seem great to others but it should be the zeal that drives you each day. Every great vision will cause others to laugh at you. Your vision should make you live beyond your natural ability.

THE VALUE YOU PLACE ON YOUR VISION DETERMINES THE ALTITUDE YOU WANT TO REACH IN LIFE.

Many great visions are dead because, the dreamer fails to run with it. Refuse to let temporary impediments distract your focal point of seeing your divine destiny come to fulfilment.

4. ATTAIN THE VISION

It is very important to write, define and run with the vision, but without attaining the vision is like chasing after the wind. There are many starters but not a lot of finishers. You have to finish everything you start in life. It is also necessary to know that it is not starting first that guarantees you success but being able to finish the race. God will not give you a vision that you cannot accomplish.

> *I have fought the good fight, I have finished the race, I have kept the faith.*
>
> 2 Timothy 4:7

History proves that, the world only crowns people who endure or fight to the end. The middle of the road is not your destination. The importance of every matter is the end results. Your vision is connected to the destinies of other

37

people and once you give up, you have killed the dreams of many people in this world.

Take a close look at all the things that help humanity to access life, how would the world be if all of those people who invented them had given up at certain point in life?

Reach your vision because your life does not lie in your beginning but your results. Regardless of all the obstacles Joseph faced, he fought the fight, run the race and brought his vision to a perfect place.

Every clear vision requires:

i. STAYING FOCUSED

One of greatest aspect of every successful person is the ability to continually see the big picture, the end result, the complete goal, even in the face of adversities. Staying focused is one of the vital keys to achieving every goal in life. Every vision God places on a man requires staying focussed.

What you focus on can have a very big impact on you whether positively or negatively. Many people have the potential to achieve great dreams in life but when the road gets tough, they tend to lose focus on the bigger picture.

The account of Nehemiah also portrays a man who stood strong and focused on his vision despite all the opposition that arose against him. Problems and challenges will always arise. But, you have to stay focused.

To stay focused when the road becomes challenging, it is important one keeps these vital keys in mind;

1. Focus on the vision not on your mistakes (Philippians 3:13-14).
2. Focus on the promises of God not the problems (2 Peter 1:4).

3. Focus on thanking God every day for everything that happens in your life (Romans 8:38).

There are many times you might feel discouraged, but it is important you hold onto the word of God.

Joseph's family did not like his dream. He had much opposition because of his dream. He also faced many challenges which people might define as impossible to overcome but he stood firm and focused on God and did not allow any impediments to stand in his way.

He focused on the promise of God concerning his life. The Bible says if God be for us who can be against us (Romans 8:31). The storms will come but keep focusing on the assignment and once you do not take your eyes of the vision.

ii. PRAYER

Every God-given vision requires constant prayer. Prayer simply means, communicating with God and developing to be one with him.

To be one with God means, your purpose, vision and reasoning is one with His. Prayer is the foundation of building a closer intimacy with God.

One of the influential things known in successful people is their commitment to prayer. The Bible teaches us to pray without ceasing (1 Thessalonians 5:17).

'PRAYER WITHOUT HAVING A RELATIONSHIP WITH GOD IS AS POWERLESS AS AN EMPTY VESSEL.'

Prayer helps you to know what to do whiles pursuing your goal. Prayer also keeps you focus in times of trials and challenges. Many people have made prayer to be a daily routine. The issue is that, it loses its efficacy when it becomes a religious formality. Prayer is not just asking God to do something. One aspect of prayer is also worshipping and praising God (1 Thessalonians 5:16-18).

Prayer is also exercising your legal right as a child of God on earth. To know God also comes through prayer. To access God's power and His resources requires earnest prayer. It is not just any prayer. It is earnest prayer that brings victory over the enemy.

> *Therefore confess your sins to each other and pray for each other so that you may be healed. The prayer of a righteous person is powerful and effective.*
>
> James 5:16

Many people do not pray along this line but they are expectant of their prayers. Pray earnestly for your vision and commit every plan on your way into the hands of God. The moment you embrace and recognize the truth of praying earnestly, you will be more fruitful in all vicinity of your abilities. It is vital to have constant fellowship with God to function more efficiently, otherwise your dream will not materialize.

iii. FASTING

Fasting literally signifies abstaining from food for spiritual reason. Specifically, submitting ourselves to deny the things that give satisfaction to the flesh such as food, drink, sleep, or sex for spiritual strength.

Spiritual fasting is not just abstaining from food but is an act of obedience to God. Fasting removes the distractions from our lives. We live in a world where we are distracted by many things.

When Nehemiah had the vision to rebuild the walls of Jerusalem, he did not only pray but also fasted. Prayer is always associated with fasting. When you fast it brings total dependence on God. (Nehemiah 1:4).

Fasting should not be considered as a way of losing weight or a dieting method. Fasting is a spiritual principle but not something you do to gain recognition.. The Bible says, 'When you fast, do not look somber as the hypocrites do, for they disfigure their faces to show others they are fasting' (Mathew 6:16).

PRINCIPLE 5

PASSION

Passion is your first step to achievement. It is one of the most influential keys needed to unlock the door to your greatness. Passion is not just having a mere desire. In fact, passion is the most dominant desire a man can possess.

Many people have the desire to achieve great things but they do not have the passion to bringing to a complete finish. They wish to do great things in life but they are not passionate about them. Passion transcends beyond desire. Passion is what creates zeal to move forward when the road becomes stiff. Passion is the fuel that pushes you to the realization of your dreams.

HOW HUNGRY YOU ARE DETERMINES THE ALTITUDE YOU ARE WILLING TO TRAVEL IN ORDER TO ACHIEVE YOUR DREAMS AND GOALS.

I have never met anyone in life who accidentally woke up and found themselves in the positions they are. Any great achievement or success does not just happen. Everyone must have the passionate desire; that is your willingness to succeed must be bigger than your desire. You cannot live without it.

But if I say, "I will not mention his word or speak anymore in his name," his word in my heart like a fire, a fire shut up in my bones. I am weary of holding it in; indeed, I cannot.

Jeremiah 20:9

The burning sensation in your bones that keep you focus, gives you the drive to move on when you are hit with setbacks, that say you cannot sit down, those voices in you that says you can make so keep on keeping on, is what is referred as PASSION.

PASSION IS A DOMINANT CHARACTER THAT GIVES YOU THE ENERGY TO OVERCOME ALL OBSTACLES IN REACHING YOUR DREAMS AND GOALS IN LIFE.

Joseph was a man with a passionate desire to fulfil the plan of God concerning his life. Joseph did not only dream, but he was passionate about seeing his dream come to life. There is no reference to Joseph been born into a rich family yet he succeeded where many people have failed. Wrong thoughts have led many people to believe that born into a rich family or Europe automatically makes one successful. If so then there will be many successful people in the world but the truth is far different from believing that theology.

What caused common men and women born into poor countries, dysfunctional homes, sicknesses and many more to achieve their dreams in life?

In a simple word: PASSION.

They started like everyone else but what distinct them was their true attitude of constant PASSIONATE DESIRE.

Joseph had a dream. He wanted to make a difference in the life of people. His dream sounded impossible as a shepherd boy to become a prime minister. Joseph wanted this so strong that he could even live for a minute without thinking about his dream.

When you are passionate about your dream, three things must happen:

1. PASSION WILL INCREASE YOUR WILLPOWER

Joseph had a dream. He wanted to be in a position where he could make great influence in people's life. He was passionate about his dream that he could not stop talking about his dream to his brothers.

When you are impregnated with dream, the burning desire in your heart will not allow you to keep silent.

The Bible states, "a good man brings good things out of the good stored up in his heart, and an evil man brings evil things out of the evil stored up in his heart. For the mouth speaks what the heart is full of (Luke 6:45)."

What is in your heart will always come out and will also bear fruit. It is also vital to watch what comes out from your mouth and the people you share your dream with.

2. PASSION WILL INCREASE YOUR VISION POWER

Passion will cause you to see your dream in a higher dimension. It will draw you closer to your dream.

Joseph understood the power of visualizing his dream before it materialised. How well you are able to see determines how far you are willing to go. Joseph knew his dream would come to pass at all cost because he could not only feel it but could see it happening one day.

There is also a true statement that, what you see determines what you pursue. He saw it before it happen. He saw what all his family could not see.

Do you see yourself as the person God says or you see what others say about you?

Joseph refused to see what others see about him. They saw a shepherd boy but he saw a shepherd boy who will one day become a prime minister.

WHEN YOU CAN VISUALISE WHAT OTHERS CANNOT SEE ABOUT YOU, IT WILL GIVE YOU THE POWER TO MOVE CLOSER TO YOUR DREAM.

3. PASSION WILL GIVE YOU THE ENERGY TO OWN YOUR DREAM.

When you cherish something, the best possible thing you can do is to protect it with all your heart. The Bible confirms that, for where your treasure is, there your heart will be also (Mathew 6:21).

Joseph heard the word and he kept it with all his strength. He knew the value of the word God had spoken into his spirit. He pursued his dream with all his heart. He believed it and owned it. He possessed his dream and took every step to protect it.

It is your responsibility to keep your dream and protect it with all your heart without allowing the enemy to steal and destroy it.

Joseph demonstrated the power of passion. When you develop passion to achieve something, it becomes part of who you are. You talk about it, sleep with and eat with it. It literally becomes part and parcel of you.

Your willingness to achieve your dream is determined by how passionate you are about bringing it to pass. Passion will give you the energy to keep doing what you like doing best all the time. Joseph was passionate about his dream and made it through till the end and you can do the same.

Martin Luther King Jr once said;

"If a man is called to be a street sweeper, he should sweep streets even as Michelangelo painted, or Beethoven composed music, or Shakespeare wrote poetry. He should sweep streets so well that all the hosts of heaven and earth will pause to say, here lived a great street sweeper who did his job well."

PRINCIPLE **6**

RENEWING YOUR MIND

And do not be conform to this world but be transform by the renewing of your mind that you
Romans 12:2

Your mind is the most essential facility or key you have in your pursuit of accomplishing your dreams and goals in life. Your mind has the power to affect you positive or negative depending on the information you receive. An indecisive person is double-minded and unstable in all his ways (James 1:8). It is easy to be distracted by the issues of life when our mind is not set on the word of God and been renewed always.

TRUE SUCCESS AND GREAT ACHIEVEMENTS BEGINS AS AN IMAGINATION FROM THE MIND.

Renewing your mind is the ability to eliminate every negative thought. Family, friends, media and the world have certain way they want people to conform with so is vital to monitor and control the source of your information. Your thoughts are very important because they shape your life. Many people have experienced hurt, disappointments, failures and have allowed the thought of negativity to rule their lives.

WHEN YOUR MIND IS FILLED WITH NEGATIVE THOUGHTS, YOU ARE ATTRACTED TO THINGS THAT CAN DISTRACT YOU FROM PURSUING YOUR DREAMS AND GOALS IN LIFE.

Joseph lived with his family who told him to forget his dream. He had a choice to believe and accept what he was told by his family. You have the ability to believe, choose and reject what you hear and what you can see. Joseph chose to control his thoughts and keep the seed (dream) of God in his spirit.

> *Finally, brothers, whatever is true, whatever is noble, whatever is right, whatever is pure, whatever is lovely, whatever is admirable--if anything is excellent or praiseworthy--think about such things.*
>
> Philippians 4:8

Renewing your mind is a constant process. It is something you are going to do for the rest of your life if you want constant blessing. Joseph accepted the thought of prosperity, success and joy by constantly renewing his mind on the word of God. Your mind is very powerful tool that can influence every area of success.

> *The weapons we fight with are not the weapons of the world. On the contrary, they have divine power to demolish strongholds. We demolish arguments and every pretension that sets itself up against the knowledge of God, and we take captive every thought to make it obedient to Christ.*
>
> 2 Corinthians 10:4-5

Strongholds are thoughts designed to pull one down. Many born again Christians are still captive to the world because they fail to keep renewing their mind.

Your spirit is saved when you are born again not your soul and body. It is important you keep renewing the mind to overcome the issues of the past because the enemy will always throw them back into your mind.

The mind is like a compass that directs the body. The information you receive is what the mind processes.

The enemy will always project the spirit of fear, doubt, unbelief, self-defeating attitude and many more into your mind. When the devil defeats you in the mind, then he knows he has already won the battle.

PEOPLE WHO THINK THEY ARE BEATEN ARE THOSE WHO PULL THE PLUG BEFORE THEY EVEN START THE FIGHT. WINNING STARTS FROM THE MIND.

All that the enemy wants to hear is when you say I cannot make it, it is impossible, am tired, am not worth this, forget it and then pull the plug. He knows our thoughts can create a strong belief.

Some of our beliefs are formed during our childhood years and they still continue to have great impacts in our lives today. Positive thoughts as well as negative thoughts have the ability to produce fruits. Anyone who conceives negative will achieve negative and who conceive positive will achieve positive. The Bible says, 'as a man thinks so he is.' (Proverbs 23:7)

"YOUR THOUGHTS ARE THE BUILDERS OF YOUR DREAM"

The environment you exhibit is very important. The environment is made up of things we can see, touch and feel and those we cannot see. If your environment is not conducive, there is a probability your dream will be destroy due to negative voices that surround you.

Sometimes what is taking place on the inside of you is different from what is happening outside. The outside is saying is impossible, your age is catching up and all you can

see is signs of discouragement but the inside is telling you
there is hope. This is because your inward man is renewed
day by day (2 Corinthians 4:16).

Many Christians are infuriated because they are
fulfilling other people's dreams instead of theirs. It is
important to know the source of your dream because not
every dream is from God. The most important reason why
you have to keep renewing your mind is to able to test what
is good, what is pleasing to God and His will concerning your
life. Without knowing this, one is bound to live in the world
of disaster. It is your responsibility to test whether your
dream is from God through His word.

> *Every good and perfect gift is from above, coming down
> from the Father of the heavenly lights, who does not change
> like shifting shadows.*

James 1:17

Joseph knew his dream was from God. He kept
renewing his mind to overcome all negativity, which would
have become impediments to achieving his dream and you
have the power to do the same. Nobody can destroy your
dream if you keep the right mind-set. If you are going to
succeed and prosper your mind serves as a tool. Your mind
is the key to your breakthrough.

**"IN THE ENVIRONMENT OF A SOUND MIND,
GREATNESS GIVES BIRTH".**

PRINCIPLE 7

BE DETERMINED

You need to persevere so that when you have done the will of God, you will receive what he has promised.

Hebrews 10:36

Determination is the fuel that energizes one to pursue a greater call or divine purpose in life. It is one of the most essential values you need to develop in order to reach your goal. Your persistence to be determined to accomplishing your goals and dreams in life is very essential. It has been instituted that, one of the reasons why many people fail to accomplish their God-given dream is their inability to keep on when huddles and challenges of life shows up.

There will be many times life will get tough, you will feel exhausted, when you do not know what to do, when you feel all hope is gone and want to quit and do something else but the ability to persist is your willingness to fight to the end. Always know that determination is one of the most significant keys that will change your perception and give you the strength to focus on your dream.

Do you not know that those who run in a race all run, but one receives the prize? Run in such a way that you may obtain it. And everyone who competes for the prize is

*temperate in all things. Now they do it to obtain a
perishable crown, but we for an imperishable crown.*

1 Corinthians 9:24-25

Your great opportunity will always lie ahead of you
when you are willing to endure to the end. Denis Waitley
said, "Determination gives you the resolve to keep going in
spite of the roadblocks that lay before you." People who
understand their purpose in life never give up easily. They
bounce back with new strength when they fall because they
know where they derive their strength from.

*Many are the afflictions of the righteousbut the Lord delivers
him out of it all.*

Psalm 34:19

Determination helps you to rise above discouragement.
Joseph's spirit of determination brought his race to a perfect
completion regardless to all the difficulties he faced. Are you
determined to finish despites all the challenges and other
factors demanding you to give up?

I would like to share with you one of the greatest
personalities in the Bible called Nehemiah who I describe as
a man of determination. Nehemiah discovered the walls of
Jerusalem were broken. He had a vision of rebuilding the walls
of Jerusalem, but what was the essence of rebuilding the walls?

A dream cannot be accomplish where there is no vision.
His dream was to see the walls once again but he understood
the vision behind the rebuilding of the walls. He knew that
the walls represented God's protection concerning his
children. When nation's walls are broken down, they become
defenseless and vulnerable.

*I also told them about the gracious hand of my God on me
and what the king had said to me. They replied, "Let us start
rebuilding." So they began this good work.*

Nehemiah 2:18

51

The Bible makes it clear he withstood many challenges in his pursuit of this vision. The Bible states in the book of Nehemiah that, when Samballat, Tobiah and Ammonite heard that he had started restoring the walls of Jerusalem, they were angry and stood against his vision. Nehemiah's vision caused ordinary people to laugh and mocked him because of their short sightedness.

Your big dream should allow certain people to question whether it is possible to materialize. Through determination, he put all these men to shame.

Nehemiah understood his vision and it influenced every decision he made. He understood his dream and the vision behind it. He was determined to accomplish his vision and he stood strongly against all criticisms to face all kinds of difficulties and rose above his limitations.

The Brooklyn Bridge

In 1883, John Roebling, an innovative engineer, invented an idea of constructing a bridge connecting New York with the Long Island. He was told by expects throughout the world to forget his impossible dream. His willingness to see such dream fulfilled did not allow him to give up. His son Washington, who was an upcoming engineer, agreed to oin his father to accomplish what was described as an unimaginable task.

Shortly after construction began, an accident led to the death of John Roebling and Washington in the hospital with a brain damage, unable to talk, walk and even move.

Yet the dream did not end there.

Washington was able develop a mode of communication with the other engineers, through his wife, when he realized he could move one if his fingers. He used the method of tapping a code for his wife, explaining what he wanted the engineers to do.

For 13 years, Washington used the same method until the bridge was finally completed.

Are you facing people who are saying your dream is crazy and impossible to achieve? Today Brooklyn Bridge stands as one of the greatest bridges in the world thanks to one man's indisputable spirit and his determination to overcome every obstacle. The journey of life is filled with difficulties that can knock you down in a twinkle of an eye. With the spirit of determination and persistence, Brooklyn Bridge shows us that even dreams that seem outrageous can be accomplish.

> For everything that was written in the past was written to teach us, so that through the endurance taught in the Scriptures and the encouragement they provide we might have hope.
>
> Romans 15:4

A God-given dream will give birth to your expectations. Many of us would have thrown in the towel but Joseph, Nehemiah, Daniel and other great heroes in the Bible did not despite all the obstacles and the oppositions that stood against them. Determination will always give you the strength to overcome every limitation when you are willing to persist till you achieve your dream.

PRINCIPLE 8

BREAKING OUT OF YOUR COMFORT ZONE

"ONE OF OUR BIGGEST OBSTACLES TO ACHIEVING
OUR DREAMS IN LIFE IS OUR INABILITY TO LEAVE
OUR COMFORT ZONES"

The Comfort Zone is a behavioral state within which a person operates in an anxiety-neutral condition, using a limited set of behaviors to deliver a steady level of performance, usually without a sense of risk. The Comfort Zone also refers to the set of environments and behaviors with which someone feels comfortable, without appreciating a sense of risk. A person's disposition can be described by his or her Comfort Zones.

We all have Comfort Zones. A Comfort Zone is anything that allows you to feel comfortable and think that you do not deserve to change or maximize your potential. We experience less pains and failures; however, we cannot achieve anything great when we choose to live in our Comfort Zones.

T. Harv Eker's quote:

"Nobody ever died of discomfort yet living in the name of discomfort has killed more ideas, more opportunities, more actions, and more growth than everything else combine.

Comfort Kills!

Have you wondered why there are six billion people in this world but only few are able to achieve their potential in life? Research shows that 97% of people in this world with great potentials to achieve their dreams are still living in their comfort zones. Only 3% are those who stretch to achieve their dreams.

This has caused many people to bury their great dreams without any manifestation in life. You are right to say that you have improved when you look back from two to three years ago but what God has deposited in you is bigger than what you have at the present. Most people are achieving below their potential because they have developed the spirit of stagnation.

Thomas Edison's quote:

"We shall have no better condition in the future if we are satisfied with all those which we have at present."

God has created the world such that, everything that has life, has to grow. Growth simply means change. Many people do not see transformation in their lives, whether academically, financially or spiritually because; they are stuck in their comfort zones. This is why only a few people are able to stretch out their comfort to achieve greatness in this world. If you have a dream of making an impact on this world, do not let the devil deceive you into thinking that your present condition is better than your future.

The life of Joseph showed a man who was willing to leave his comfort zone to endure all kinds of afflictions to achieve his dream.

YOUR TRUE SUCCESS WILL BE DETERMINED WHEN YOU ARE WILLING TO STRETCH BEYOND YOUR BOUNDARIES OF COMFORT ZONE.

The Bible records that Joseph found favour in the sight

of his master. He was treated very well and his master entrusted him with everything he possessed. He could have chosen to sleep with his master's wife to continue enjoying his temporary happiness but he instead chose to obey the commandment of God to suffer persecution in order to fulfil his dream. Joseph knew that his future looked brighter than his today. Many of us fail to recognise this. If one cannot see the bigger plan of God concerning their life, there is a great risk of falling for anything along the road to divine fulfilment.

Moses is another great man in history of the Bible. He left his position as a leader in the palace when he realized he was not an Egyptian. Moses was raised in the palace and was treated as a son of Pharaoh. He had always believed he was a prince. For the purpose of God to come to pass concerning his life, he had to make a decision whether to enjoy his Comfort Zone as a prince or chose to be a slave like his brethren. He made the right decision by choosing to become a slave and that brought the promise of God to pass. Choices will always be presented but it is your responsibility to make the right decision.

Abraham is another example of a man who left his Comfort Zone. Imagine you have spent most of your life living with your family and had to leave them to settle in a foreign land where you do not know anyone there.

How does it sound?

There is a feeling of uncertainty, the discomfort of adapting to new environment, as well as missing of family and love ones and many more. This is scary especially when you do not know when you are going to see them again. The blessings of God does not come easily even through it is by His grace. We have to act in the instructions of God. Most people would have said no YET Abraham departed without questioning God, complaining or murmuring or showing any form of procrastination.

There is nothing worse than saying goodbye to the people you love. He left his father's house even though that was his place of comfort. Abraham knew that the calling of God was not just an accidental but was for a purpose which was greater than the things in his father's house or country.

IT IS BETTER TO SUFFER TEMPORARY AFFLICTION TO ACHIEVE YOUR DREAM THAN TO ENJOY TEMPORARY HAPPINESS AND THEN LIVE IN PAINFUL MEMORIES FOR THE REST OF YOUR LIFE.

Joseph left the palace of Potiphar to prison which denounced him of his temporary comfort to achieve his dream. Moses refused to be called a son of Pharaoh's daughter and chose to suffer afflictions with the children of God (Hebrew 11:24-25).

Abraham also left his father's house, which was his place of security, in order to receive the promises of God. There are many more.

What has God said to you?

If has God deposited something in you, then rise and begin to act. Your time to a rise and shine is now. (Isaiah 61:1).

PRINCIPLE 9

IDENTIFYING OPPORTUNITIES

Dreamers have an insight and wisdom to discern and the sensitivity to recognize every opportunity God brings in their lives. We live in a world full of great opportunities but being unable to identify and tap into them will cause you to miss many great things in life. Successful people are able to recognize opportunity in the midst of adversities.

> **WHAT DEFINES A VISIONARY PERSON FROM AN ORDINARY PERSON IS THE ABILITY TO SEE BEYOND IMAGINATIONS AND REACHING OUT TO THEM.**

In spite of all the challenges and the adversities Joseph went through, he utilized every opportunity that came his way. He saw his problems as opportunities.

Are you able to identify opportunities in the midst of challenges and trials?

Many opportunities do not sometimes appear as opportunities and remain hidden.

TYPES OF OPPORTUNITIES

There are many different types of opportunities. The first opportunity to be mindful of is,

1. A ONE-TIME OPPORTUNITY

There is a strong belief that, some opportunities 'come but once in a life time'. Because of this you have to be mindful and be ready to grab every chance that comes your way.

Many people do not believe this, but the truth is some opportunities will knock on your door only once in your life time. Let me share some important scenarios that will show you one time opportunities in order to be more careful of them.

i. THE WOMAN WITH THE ISSUE OF BLOOD

In the book of Mark 5:25-34, the Bible tells a story of Jesus and the woman who had issue of blood for thirty eight years. The Bible says the woman was healed after touching Jesus' garment. Through her faith, determination and perseverance, she made it by touching the garment of Jesus.

Why was she so eager to touch Jesus' garment that time? Was there not going to be another time?

What motivated her to keep her faith, determination and the spirit of perseverance was that she realised Jesus was just a PASSING OPPORTUNITY. She knew if she let Jesus go without reaching to him that would have been the end of finding cure for her issue.

ii. THE TWO CRIMINALS ON THE CROSS (Luke 23:39)

The two criminals had the opportunity to meet Jesus at the same time on the cross and they also had the opportunity to say something to Jesus. One spoke foolishly but the other said something that moved the heart of Jesus. Maybe, they had messed their life up but the fact they all had the opportunity to speak to Jesus was a once in a life chance to be with Jesus in Heaven. One seized the moment and the other threw away his chance. This also teaches us to watch when to talk and be careful with what we say.

iii. THE BLIND BARTIMAEUS (Mark 10:46-52)

The blind Bartimaeus was so determined to receive his healing regardless of how the crowd shouted at him to keep quiet. The Bible says he kept shouting the more they asked him to shut up. He had been blind since birth yet was the only one who knew Jesus was from David's lineage. The man was a person with revelation despite his limitation. He did not want anything to stop his blessing because he understood his moment was a passing opportunity. He did not know when he was going to meet Jesus again.

There are many examples in the Bible such as the five foolish virgins (Mathew 25:1-13), the parable of the banquet (Luke 14:16-24) and many more. You can have a great attitude to achieving in life but being unable to identify such opportunity will hinder you from achieving your true potential in life.

2. OPPORTUNITY THROUGH TALENT

Being imprisoned for no reason, Joseph had every right to feel betrayed by people. He had a dream but all the evidence before him showed that he was going in the opposite direction. However, he was able to identify an opportunity in the prison. He stopped focusing on himself and instead focused on how he can utilise his talent to be a blessing for the prisoners. Soon he was seen as a different man and his gift began to create opportunities for him whiles in jail.

God has crafted all mankind with great talents to accomplish something in this world. Any gift or talent you have, use it to your advantage. Your talent will open closed doors. What are you going through that makes you feel all hope is gone?

A gift opens the way and ushers the giver into the presence of the great.

Proverbs 16:18

While Joseph suffered in prison he met two chief servants from King Pharaoh's house. These two butlers had dreams but could not understand them. Something was missing here. They needed an interpreter.

Do you get the picture?

This was a BIG opportunity for Joseph because he had a gift of interpreting dreams.

Joseph asked the chief servant to recommend him to Pharaoh. This was all that Joseph wanted but did not happen so he had to spend another two years in prison. This could seen as a failure but Joseph did not hold any resentment against the chief servant. Joseph knew that his gift as an interpreter can create an opportunity for him so he was always ready to grab every little chance that came his way.

SUSAN'S BOYLE STORY

How many people remember this woman? She is a Scottish singer who appeared as a contestant on the TV programme Britain's Got Talent on 11 April 2009. This is what happened when she came on the stage:

SIMON [Judge]- What's your name darling?
Susan- My name is Susan Boyle.
SIMON- Where are you from?
Susan- From Blackburn, West Lothian, Scotland.
SIMON-And how old are you Susan?
Susan- Am 47 and just one side of me.
SIMON- Ok what's the dream?

Susan-Am trying to be a professional singer.

SIMON-And why hasn't it worked out so far?

Susan-Have never been given the chance before and here whole thing else will change.

SIMON-Who do you want to be successful as?

Susan-Elaine Paige.

SIMON- What are you going to sing tonight?

Susan-Am going to sing I dream a dream from Les Miserables.

From the profiling of human archives, she was written off when the judges and the whole audience saw her. Susan recognised that was her chance (opportunity) to rise above her critics. She had already stated that she had never had the chance before. Dreamers are able to identify opportunities and give all they have to make it successful. She did not allow the preconception of the people to determine her potential.

"YOUR APPEARANCE DOES NOT DETERMINE YOUR VALUE AND WHAT YOU ARE MADE OF."

They judged her by her outward appearance and by her age. As is said, 'do not judge a book by its cover'. Almost everyone in the room laughed and mocked her however they were the same people who clapped and cheered for her when they heard her singing.

Many people are talented but keep struggling in life because of their inability to seize their opportunities. Susan knew what she had and she was not ready to miss her big opportunity.

Not only did Susan go on to become a star but she also achieved her dream by singing with her music icon Elaine Paige on 13/12/2009 on ITV1.

3. DISGUISED OPPORTUNITIES

Disguised opportunities refer to those opportunities which are not clear to see. They always hide behind the door and without insight, it is impossible to identify them. They often come in a form of a problem or challenge. Many people run away from such opportunities because it comes with paying a bigger price in order to breakthrough.

> *Opportunities are usually disguised as hard work, so most people don't recognize them.*
>
> Ann Landers

Any challenge you face in life causes you to become more cognisant of certain things and opens doors to learning self-wisdom. Most often we are not open to the opportunities that come our way because we focus more on the problem instead of taking time to pray and see any positive outcome of the problem. Joseph through his adversities attained maturity in God. He saw his brothers' selling him as a way God had designed for him to reach his final destination.

Another great character in the Bible is David. In the book of 1 Samuel 17:23-24, the Bible records the conflict between the Philistines and Israelites. Israel was a great nation but the Bible says Goliath and his armies tormented them. The Israelites ran with great fear instead of remembering God as their strength. (1 Samuel 17:11)

"DAVID SAW AN OPPORTUNITY BUT ISRAELITES SAW PROBLEM (GIANT)"

David was the youngest son of Jesse and had spent most of his life in the wilderness as a shepherd. David went to give food to his brothers on the battlefield and discovered the great tragedy that had happened to Israelites. David realised the men of Israel were afraid and running away from the problem but he saw that as an opportunity.

**THE PROBLEM THAT THREATENS TO DESTROY YOUR
LIFE IS THE VERY THING THAT WILL CAUSE YOUR
BREAKTHROUGH IN LIFE.**

David asked the men what could be given to the man
who kills Goliath (1 Samuel 17:26). David realized the
reward was great and so beautiful that he did not want to
miss the opportunity. To be a great dreamer, you have to
rise above difficulty to discern every opportunity that comes
in your life.

4. CREATIVE OR ENGINEERED OPPORTUNITIES

People with creative minds will always be open to creating
opportunity for themselves when it seems all doors are
closed. One of my favourite characters in the Bible is
Zacchaeus. The Bible recalls Zacchaeus as a chief tax
collector, a wealthy man. However, his limitation was his
height. Jesus was passing through Jericho and Zacchaeus
wanted to see him, but could not because the crowd had
gone ahead of him.

Zacchaeus strategically positioned himself by creating
a unique opportunity. He climbed the sycamore tree so that
Jesus could see him. When Jesus reached there, he looked
up and said, "Zacchaeus come down immediately for I must
stay in your home today."

> *Opportunity rarely knocks on your door. Knock rather on
> opportunity's door if you ardently wish to enter.*
> B.C. Forbes

The most interesting part of this story is that Zacchaeus
was trying to reach out to Jesus but after tactically
positioning himself well, Jesus went to him. Always know
that the world has room for people who show what they
capable of doing.

What motivated Zacchaeus to contrive such an opportunity?

i. IT WAS A PASSING OPPORTUNITY

Zacchaeus had insight to understand that Jesus was passing through Jericho was not just an accident but for a purpose. Allowing Jesus to pass without reaching out to him meant he would have lost a great opportunity because he did not know when Jesus would pass through Jericho again.

ii. HE IDENTIFIED HIS OWN OBSTACLES

We all have limitations or obstacles which we do not want other people to see. Zacchaeus did not allow his obstacles to stop him. Until we are able to recognize and disregard our limitations, we will miss many opportunities that come our way.

WHAT YOU CHOOSE TO THINK AND BELIEVE DETERMINE THE OUTCOME OF YOUR ACTIONS.

Learn to overlook every limitation in your life and create your own unique opportunities. Your height or stature does not determine your future.

iii. HE REFUSED TO FOLLOW THE CROWD

Many people are chasing the wind in life. As long as the wind blows they are ready to follow. Zacchaeus refused to be like everyone else. He thought differently and decided differently.

A MAN WHO KNOWS HIS DIRECTION IN LIFE HAS THE UNDERSTANDING OF WHERE HE IS GOING AND WHERE HE IS COMING FROM.

Zacchaeus did not just run like everyone. He ran with

a goal in mind to achieve a purpose. He chose to position himself well to receive what he required. He created a way that the opportunity found him rather than him pursuing the opportunity (1 Corinthians 9:26).

People will not understand why God has chosen you. You might not be good as other people, talented, gorgeous and educated but refuse to be defined by people and refuse to follow the crowd. Zacchaeus imagined it and created his opportunity when no one understood what he was doing.

THE DECISION YOU TAKE TODAY DETERMINES YOUR TOMORROW OR FUTURE.

5. DANGEROUS OPPORTUNITY

This opportunity is not one of those great opportunities that open doors for you to pursue your God-given dream but instead it acts to obstruct your focus and destroy your divine destiny. This kind of opportunity often appears beautiful and easy to figure out but dangerous.

Have you ever been in need of something so badly that you thought of taking a short cut?

Think about all the big ideas that appeared up in your mind; they seemed very reasonable to solving your issues but was it God's plan? Good ideas are not always God's ideas. Let me share with you some examples of dangerous opportunity in order to be more attentive about them when they appear:

i. JOSEPH AND POTIPHAR'S WIFE

The Bible describes Joseph as a very handsome young man. Potiphar's wife took notice of Joseph and presented him a great offer. Joseph knew it was not a good opportunity. It was not AN opportunity to lead him to his

God's divine purpose but, instead, to destroy him. The Bible states, 'the thief comes only to steal and kill and destroy; I have come that they may have life, and have it to the full' (John 9:10).

It is always great to be young and energetic but it is also a perilous time because the devil will present many opportunities to you and all the pleasures of life during this age. Joseph was a wise man who had an insight to reject such an opportunity. He remembered his God while he was young. (Ecclesiastes 12:1)

iii. DAVID AND SAUL (1 Samuel 26:2-3, 7-11)

David was anointed to become the next King of Israel. King Saul turned against David and pursued him many times to kill him. Thanks be to God, as many would have said, David had many great opportunities to kill King Saul. There was an opportunity for David to kill King Saul and to be enthroned sooner. However, he knew killing Saul was not a good opportunity. David knew Saul was anointed of God and touching him would have brought the wrath of God upon himself.

Also in the book of 2 Samuel 11:2-4, When David was a king; he was standing on the balcony when he saw Sheba. David thought that was a good opportunity to kill her husband and take her beautiful wife without knowing it was a dangerous opportunity that the devil had offered him. David sinned against God and paid the consequences for that.

THE ANOINTING OF GOD WILL EITHER MAKE YOU OR BREAK YOU DEPENDING ON HOW YOU UTILISE IT.

iv. THE FORBIDDEN FRUIT IN THE GARDEN OF EDEN

Now the serpent was more crafty than any of the wild animals the LORD God had made. He said to the woman, "Did God really say, 'You must not eat from any tree in the garden'?"

Genesis 3:1

The devil misled Eve to believe that, eating the fruit God had instructed them not to eat was not really wrong. Eve thought that was a fantastic opportunity because the enemy said she would know what was good and evil and man would be like God.

What the devil said to Eve was a fact. Facts are not truths. That was not how God had intended for man to live. The deal seemed good but was a dangerous opportunity that led to opening the door to sin in the world and all the painful things man is experiencing. Opportunity might look good on the outside but that does not determine the value of it.

6. OPPORTUNITIES THROUGH GIVING

One way to identify opportunity is to give. Giving is one of the most profound principles in the Bible that assures constant increase in your life. Many people receive all the time but find it hard to give. Giving here does not necessary mean money but ANYTHING. Giving can also be in sharing your belongings, your faith and your time with others to promote the Kingdom of God.

Give and it will be given to you. A good measure, pressed down, shaken together and running over, will be poured . into your lap. For with the measure you use, it will be measured to you

Luke 6:38

Giving always creates a way to facilitate your receiving,

for one cannot receive without first giving. The Bible teaches us to give from our heart and the more we give the more we will receive. God gave his only begotten son to the world so that He might gain the heart of many who will believe in him.

> *For God so loved the world that he gave his one and only*
> *Son, that whoever believes in him shall not perish but have*
> *eternal life.*
>
> John 3:16

Giving creates an opportunity to receive more blessings. These are examples of people who gave in the Bible and through their giving received great blessings.

    i. Abraham invited the three strangers into his house. He gave them water, washed their feet and fed them as their custom demanded. Through his hospitality, he received a confirmation of the covenant God had already made to him that he would have a promise son and will become a great nation (Genesis 18:1-15).

   II. The Shunamite woman was able to identify the needs of prophet Elijah and gave him a place to sleep. Her generosity to Prophet Elijah opened an opportunity for her to have a child and also all her assets were restored back to her by the king (2 kings 4:8-10, 6:8).

  iii. The boy released the five loaves of bread and two fishes which brought the miracle of feeding the five thousand people who were with Jesus. Until you have released what is in your hand, God cannot work on your behalf. Do not be stingy (Luke 6:5-12).

  iv. The widow did not have enough oil in her house. She refused to eat with her children alone but shared all the oil she had in her house with Prophet Elijah and she never lacked oil again. Sharing brings an increase (2 Kings 4:1-7).

Understand the principle of giving.

WHAT YOU GIVE TO THIS WORLD IS WHAT YOU GET AND THE MEASURE IN WHICH YOU GIVE DETERMINES THE MEASURE WITH WHICH YOU WILL RECEIVE.

Always be encouraged to give more, for giving is the secret of receiving and living in the overflow or abundance of God's blessings.

7. OPPORTUNITY THROUGH RECOMMENDATION

Opportunity through recommendation is another type of opportunity that comes as a result of someone recommending you because of the Godly Character you have demonstrated. Also one can be recommended for his or her diligent work. Another way which one can be recommended is when one possesses a unique gift or talent that can be of great use for society, companies, or the world.

Also one can recommend you because of some kindness you have shown to them. Anything you do, it is always important we do it well because we do not know who is watching us.

Some examples of opportunity through recommendation are these:

- Joseph was recommended to King Pharaoh because of his unique talent and his character to love and forgive everyone. He held no grudge even when the chief butler forgot about him for two years.
- The Shunamite woman in the book of 2 Kings was recommended to the king by Gehazi because of her hospitality to Elisha, the servant of God.

- David was recommended not because he was anointed of God but his ability to play the harp to drive evil spirits from King Saul.
- Jeroboam was also recommended to King Solomon in 1 Kings because he was noted as a brave man and very industrious.

8. DIVINE OPPORTUNITIES

Divine opportunities are those kind of opportunities that are ordained and plan by God through his grace. When the spirit of God is present on a man's life, it opens many doors for him. A divine opportunity always comes with impacting the life of others in a positive manner. It eliminates self-centeredness and is always for God's glorification.

God has his own way of creating an opportunity for people. Many great heroes such as Abraham, Joseph, Prophet Daniel, King David, Nehemiah, Jeremiah, Paul and many more realized their divine opportunities and took steps to pursue the path of their God- given purposes.

Regardless of how many opportunities you have missed in life, God can still make a way for you. Be sensitive to recognize when God bring such an opportunity into your life. Divine opportunity requires four things.

i. Absolute obedience to God.
ii. Recognition.
iii. Total trust and Confidence in God.
iv. Humility.

"When one door of happiness closes, another opens; but often we look so long at the closed door that we do not see the one which has been opened for us."
Helen Keller

Many great opportunities have been missed but God can give you more great opportunities to make more impact in the life of others if you are willing to seize and utilize them. Opportunities are open doors God uses to elevate people to fulfilling their purpose in life.

PRINCIPLE 10

PAYING THE PRICE

Any achievement in life with great value has a price that must be paid. If you are willing to succeed then you must be willing to pay the price. Most people have big dreams and goals in life, they end up giving up because they failed to pay the price to see their dream materialize.

It is important to know that while we deal with major obstacles in our journey to fulfill our dreams and goals, there is also a greater price to pay. There is no crown without paying a price.

> *Do you not know that in a race all the runners run, but only one gets the prize? Run in such a way as to get the prize.*
>
> 1 Corinthians 9:24

Every dream that God deposits in you will come to pass if you are willing to pay the price. All the great heroes in the Bible had to pay the price to reach their God-given purposes.

THE PRICE YOU PAY DETERMINES THE QUALITY AND THE SIZE OF THE DREAM GOD HAS DEPOSITED IN YOU AND HOW FAR YOU ARE WILLING TO REACH IN LIFE.

Joseph had to pay the price in order to accomplish his dream. Paying the price is a crucial moment in the life of every dreamer. A dream is just like a seed in the womb of a woman which would in due time bear forth a child. Nobody sees the child of a pregnant woman in her early years until they realise it is developing from one stage to the other.

A pregnant woman is likely to face many negative challenges before giving birth to a child. Every dreamer has to go through the same pattern. The pregnant woman has to pay the price for the seed in her womb to see her child come to reality. During the time of paying the price, these things have to be noted carefully in order to succeed.

1. AVOID ABORTION

The enemy is very clever. He will do everything in his power for you to abort the dream you are carrying just like a baby in the womb of a woman. For the pregnant woman to see her baby delivered without causing any defect to the baby, she has to pay the price for the unborn baby.

The pregnant woman sometimes has to stop eating probably her favourite food, change her dress code, where she goes and even how she talks to protect her unborn child and deliver at the right time. Many dreams, visions, and ideas have been destroyed because of the dreamer's inability to sustain the dream they are carrying.

2. AVOID PREMATURE BIRTH

When dreams are prematurely delivered the dreamer begins to struggle in many areas of his life. This is because he did not understand God's timing. Joseph did not procrastinate as a young man but valued the spiritual timing. He waited for the right time like other heroes in the Bible. Without maturity one cannot stand during times of storms and challenges of life. Wait for the right time to avoid premature birth.

3. AVOID MISCARRIAGE

Many big dreams are malfunctioning because of ignorance to accept and follow certain truths to bring them to reality. Many people have a small womb which makes it hard to contain big dreams. God-given dreams are always bigger and beyond human imagination which requires big womb.

Without enlarging your territory it is impossible to occupy what God has placed within you. Carelessness can also lead to dream miscarriage when you refuse to do the right thing. Visualize your big dream as God's dream and follow it with all your heart and deliver it.

There are also two major things that will happen during the time you have to pay the price.

1: CRITICISM

Every dreamer faces criticism from others. As a pregnant woman gets criticize for her change of character and certain actions due to the seed in her womb, so is a dreamer.

The moment Joseph announced his dream, he was criticized as an arrogant child by his brothers and even his father. They all had the same mind-set concerning Joseph. Is he going to rule over us? According to their culture and tradition, they perceived their younger brother becoming a leader over them as an insult.

Criticism does not necessarily mean that you have done something wrong. Jesus, who is our master, was criticized and rejected for doing nothing wrong. Criticism actually enlightens you to be more mindful of yourself and encourages you to learn self-wisdom.

David was criticized for been proud and arrogant when he wanted to fight Goliath. His brothers told him to g   o back home for he was too young to be at the battlefield. Confidence separates visionary people from ordinary people.

YOUR POSITION OR AGE DOES NOT DETERMINE YOUR MATURITY IN GOD BUT YOUR RIGHT STANDING AND TRUE OBEDIENCE TO HIS WORD.

2: REJECTION

Rejection is part of the package as a dreamer. You will fall into small select group of people when you begin to strive toward your dream. It is one thing you cannot ignore in your journey to achieving great success or accomplishment. Dreamers are not only rejected because people hate them but most time people do not want to associate with them due to their inability to envisage their vision.

You are going to come across some rejections in your life but be willing to face them if you want to succeed.

"We keep going back, stronger, not weaker, because we will not allow rejection to beat us down. It will only strengthen our resolve. To be successful there is no other way."

Earl E.Graves

Joseph paid the price of rejection for his dream. He was hated so badly and sold as a slave. He was rejected from the family into a foreign land, all because of his dream. David was also rejected as not qualified to fight Goliath but that gave him the resolve to trust in his God who delivered him (1 Samuel 17:37).

There are many famous people in history who have faced criticism and rejection but have stood up to become what they are today.

   i. Colonel Harlan Sanders refused rejection over 300 times but more than 15,000 KFC restaurants in 109 countries and more than 12 million customers are being serve daily.

  ii. John Creasy, a British mystery novelist, received 743 rejection slips before he sold his first book. Over the next 40 years, he went on to publish more than 600 full length books. 743 rejections until he achieved his goal.

 iii. Les brown, a well acclaimed motivational speaker was criticised and rejected many times when seeking a job at a radio station.

 iv. Martin Luther King, was a man who had big dreams and visions. He was criticised and rejected by many Americans on 28 August, 1963, when he called for racial equality and an end to discrimination.

Every meaningful dream or ambition will need a substantial price to pay in order to bring it to pass. Be willing to pay the price to see your dream come to pass to be a blessing to many generations. If you want something tangible that transcends beyond the ordinary, you must be willing and be prepared to pay the price.

PRINCIPLE 11

OVERCOMING FEAR

God has designed mankind for greater purposes but fear of failure has incapacitated many to live below the standard of their true potential. Fear of failure has imprisoned many great destinies. There are many fears in the world but fear of failure is one of the most powerful enemies that cripples people from pursuing their divine purpose.

Fear is false evidence appearing real. It is the boundary between wisdom and ignorance.

> *For God has not given us a spirit of fear, but of power and of love and of a sound mind*
> 2 Timothy 1:7

I have never met anyone who wishes to fail or decide to fail in some point of their lives. Fear of failure has become an unaccepted word that people do not want to hear in our society. Everyone wants to be successful and success has become the word engineered in people's mind. Many seminars are held, books written and other materials on how to become successful but people tend to forget that success is not in failure but failure is in success. No matter how a person becomes successful in life, he or she might have experienced failures in some point of their lives.

THE ONLY MAN WHO DOES NOT WANT TO MAKE A MISTAKE IS THE MAN WHO DOES NOT WANT TO ACCOMPLISH ANY GREAT THING.

Many people are stuck on paths to pursuing their divine dreams because they have not learnt to embrace failure as part and parcel of their journey. We are afraid to fail because failure makes us think we have let our family, friends, God and everyone down. Failure is part of life.

SOME VITAL POINTS TO CONSIDER ABOUT FEAR OF FAILURE:

- No one wants to fail.
- No one decides to fail.
- Everyone has failed.
- No one is exempted from failure.
- Everyone responds to failure differently.

We have emphasized failure to an extreme degree that everyone pretends to behave as though they are perfect. Failure does not mean you are unsuccessful. It is in the nature of man to fail since we are not God. Man has failed both spiritually and physically.

The Bible states 'that we have all sin (failed) and fall short of the glory of God'. There are many areas you have probably failed such as in relationships, business, academically, financially and many but they should not hinder you from moving on to achieve greater things in life. It does not matter how perfect you are, you are bound to make mistakes from time-to-time.

THE ROAD TO SUCCESS IS NOT EASY, IF IT IS EASY MANY PEOPLE WILL ACCOMPLISH GREAT THINGS BUT IT IS FILLED WITH MANY PITS AND VALLEYS THAT NEED DETERMINATIONS, COURAGE AND THE FOCUS TO DRIVE TILL THE END.

Joseph in no doubt would have considered himself as a failure. A young man with a big dream of becoming a Prime Minister discovers himself in a pit, sold as a slave and later sent to prison. But joseph understood the power of failing forward. Joseph experienced failures upon failures but stood firm. He was not moved by failure but focused on God and keeping a good attitude.

HOW YOU CHOOSE TO APPROACH YOUR OWN FAILURES WILL DETERMINE THE IMPACT ON YOUR FUTURE.

Fear of failure is one of the reasons why many will not try to utilize their talents. In Mathew 25:24-28, the parable of the talent shows, the one talent man had a negative attitude toward his master. He was afraid to fail and instead hid his talent in the ground and believing his master to approve his excuse. His master recognized him as a lazy and wicked slave and was punished.

Fear will always incapacitate you. it will stop you from discovering what you have within you. Many people have the potential to make great impact to the world but have become unproductive since they are not used for the right purpose. Fear of failure will either make you use or lose your talent.

> *Every tree that does not bear good fruit is cut down and thrown into the fire.*
> Mathew 7:19

The product of ignorance has kept many below their standard of their true potential. Many people have the ability to prosper but they are living in mediocrity as a result of fear of failure. Experiencing fear of failure is as natural as breathing. We all in times have those little feelings when we are ready to step into the unknown environment.

A study of Bible characters shows that most great men who made history were men who failed severely at some point, but shook the dust of their feet and moved on. Examples of these heroes are:

1. Abraham, who was called a friend of God but through impatience slept with her servant.
2. David, who was a man after God's own heart refused to be on the battlefield, stayed home and committed adultery and murder.
3. Paul, who converted many souls to Christ and wrote half of the New Testament, was the man who persecuted many Christians thinking he was doing God a favour.
4. Peter who through the spirit of revelation knew who Jesus was but through self-confidence denied Jesus Christ three times.
5. Moses who spoke face-to-face with God run ahead of God's timing and killed the Egyptian and also disobeyed God by striking the rock in his anger.

These man became heroes because they recognized where they failed and moved forward. The grace of God helps mankind to make restitution for his mistakes and also gives strength to move forward. God sometimes engineers failures into our life in order for success to be accomplished. However this does not mean every failure in your life is caused by God. Some failures are the results of our own ignorance.

> *I can do all things through Christ who strengthens me.*
> Philippians 4:13

People who are on the top of the ladder did not get there with success after success

Do you recognise these famous failures in history?

1. BILL GATES – The founder of Microsoft, is one of the most well-known entrepreneur in history. However 1975, he was a Harvard University drop out. He also failed his first business called with Traf-O-Data.

2. THOMAS EDISON – He is considered as one of the most creative inventors in history. In his early years, teachers told Edison he was too stupid to learn anything'. He was also fired from his first two jobs for being non-productive. At the age of 67 Edison's business was destroyed by a fire that caused more than two billion dollars' worth of damage. The next morning, Edison looked at the ruins and said, "There is great value in disaster. All our mistakes are burned up. Thank God we can start anew." He also made 1000 unsuccessful attempts to create the first popular light bulb. This resulted in his famous quote, "I have not failed; I've just found 10,000 ways that won't work."

3. ABRAHAM LINCOLN – He was elected the 16th President of the United States of America. He received no more than 5 years of formal education throughout his life time. He had twelve major failures before being elected as a president. His failures caused him to write in a letter to his friend - 'I am now the most miserable man in living. If what I feel were equally distributed to the human family, there would be no one cheerful face on earth'.

4. HENRY FORD – Became one of the most famous and richest men in the world and was known for his ingenious assembly line, but he did not prosper immediately. He failed and went broke five times before he succeeded.

5. MICHAEL JORDAN – By acclamation, he is the

greatest basketball player in history and was noted as instrumental in popularizing the NBA around the world in the 1980s and 1990s. However, Jordan was cut from their first school basketball team. His famous words are - "I've failed over and over again in my life. That is why I succeed."

6. SOICHIRO HONDA – He was turned down by Toyota Motor Corporation for an engineering job, leaving him jobless for quite some time. Through the motivation of his neighbours, he started making his own scooters at home; he later started his own business.

7. DR BEN CARSON – At the age of 32, he became Director of Pediatric Neurosurgery at Johns Hopkins Children's Centre (JHH) in Baltimore. He is internationally recognized as a pioneer in his field for separating twins joined at the back of the head, but was not just an instant success. He grew up in a single parent home, under extreme poverty and low self-esteem. He developed a violent, uncontrollable temper. Always at the bottom of the class due to his failing grades, he was considered the 'dummy' of his class. His teachers considered him as nothing and Ben would often take an entire quiz without getting a single question right.

Successful people perceive failure as an opportunity to learn from their mistakes and move on. Unlike unsuccessful people they see failure as a permanent solution to give up in fulfilling their dreams in life.

The world's greatest achievers and leaders who have contributed tremendously to the world are ones who embraced failure and understood how failure formed part of who they were and what they achieved.

Do not be afraid to fail.

PRINCIPLE 12

WAITING ON GOD

But, beloved, do not forget this one thing, that with the Lord one day is as a thousand years, and a thousand years as one day

2 Peter 3:8, Psalm 90:4

One of the most difficult things for us seems to be learning how to wait on God's timing for his amazing promises concerning our lives. Waiting is something God designed for all His faithful children to go through. Waiting requires patience. Patience is one of the fruits of the spirit and is an important character every child of God has to possess (Galatians 5:22)

Webster's Dictionary defines patience as:

1. The state or quality of being patient; the power of suffering with fortitude; uncomplaining, endurance of evils or wrongs, as toil, pain, poverty, insult, oppression, calamity, etc.
2. The act of power of calmly or contentedly waiting for something due or hoped for forbearance.
3. Constancy in labour or application; perseverance.

Patience is easy to demonstrate when things are rosy and beautiful. Patience does not develop overnight. It is a learning process we need to go through in our decision to move forward towards our visions in life. The real test of patience is seen when God takes away the things that give us joy. The Bible motivates us to understand that trials and tests are his ways of establishing our patience.

I reckon everyone has been through the sheer impatience of having to wait to board a bus that never shows up. Another good example is waiting in traffic when you are running late to catch a flight. What are you waiting on God for? A baby, financial freedom, a new job, marriage, healing, degree and what else?

- Are you stuck in a situation where you are desperate to get out?
- Do you feel that your time will expire because your time never arrives for you to grab your chance?
- Have you tried anything in your own strength to discover answers to your special needs and cannot find any?

It is often frustrating, but the only thing to do is just to wait on God. The plan of God is to give us a long term solution to the problems we are going through.

The wise man Solomon let us understand in the book of Ecclesiastes 3:1-8 that:

A Time for Everything
3 There is a time for everything,
and a season for every activity under the heavens:
2a time to be born and a time to die,
a time to plant and a time to uproot,
3a time to kill and a time to heal,
a time to tear down and a time to build,
4a time to weep and a time to laugh,
a time to mourn and a time to dance,
5a time to scatter stones and a time to gather them,

a time to embrace and a time to refrain from embracing,
6a time to search and a time to give up,
a time to keep and a time to throw away,
7a time to tear and a time to mend,
a time to be silent and a time to speak,
8a time to love and a time to hate,
a time for war and a time for peace.

Waiting simply means trial. Any dream God gives a person requires him or her to go through a wilderness period.

The wilderness period is a period between the prophesy of your dream and its fulfilment. Waiting is one of the crucial activities in the life of every dreamer. It is the time when God will test you in many areas of your life.

The purpose of the trial is not for God to destroy or harm you but to shape you into becoming the person He requires you be to in order to handle every task he places in your hand. This is the time when your inward and outward character is developed.

Every dream God gives a person requires waiting for its due time. Most people are discouraged and consider themselves as failures due to their inability to understand God's timing. God operates at his own momentum. Our ways and plans differ from God's ways and plans and His timing is different from our timing.

> *"For my thoughts are not your thoughts, neither are your ways my ways,"* declares the LORD.
> Isaiah 55:8

Joseph waited for thirteen years before his defining moment arrived. God has a specific time for the release of His abundance blessings towards those who believe and diligently seek him. (Hebrew 11:6)

Joseph understood that knowing God's timing is a fundamental part of his journey. He refused to take short cuts to enjoy temporary happiness but rather chose to endure all kinds of afflictions to achieve his destiny.

THE INSTRUCTION YOU CHOOSE TO OBEY OF GOD DETERMINES THE FUTURE YOU CREATE.

God knows what will happen today, tomorrow and in future. He knew all things concerning our lives before we were even conceived in the womb. God knew what Joseph would go through and also knew that He is the one who will deliver him but, Joseph had to be tried by the word(Psalm 105:19).

Your testing time will determine the kind of vessel you possess. There are different kinds of vessels such as the Golden Vessel, the Silver Vessel, the Clay Vessel and the wooden vessel (1 Timothy 2:20). I can say that Joseph can be identified as a Golden Vessel because he demonstrated the attitude of willingness and purity while waiting on God despite all the odds.

THE TYPE OF VESSEL YOU POSSESS DETERMINES THE QUALITY AND THE LEVEL OF MATURITY IN YOUR WALK WITH GOD.

Waiting always shows a time of silence. It is a time you feel like God has shut the gates of heaven to your prayers. Until we stay focused and faithful to God's timing, we will never understand what God wants us to do in life. Waiting is also defined as a time of pruning.

Oxford Dictionary defines Pruning as trimming (a tree, shrub or bush) by cutting away dead or overgrown branches or stem, especially to increase fruitfulness and growth.

All God's children go through a period of pruning. It is the time when God will eliminate many unwanted things

87

that would cause distraction to us in future. All God's
children go through a period of pruning. For you to flourish
in your season and allow God to bring out the best in you,
it is important you acknowledge the usefulness of God's
timing concerning your life.

There are times in our lives when we all feel we do not
understand why we cannot do what we want to do. Yes,
pruning is a hard time but it is worth waiting on God to
accomplish His task concerning you. Do not allow anything
to crush your destiny while waiting. God will test us on
everything we ask from Him.

> *He cuts off every branch in me that bears no fruit, while
> every branch that does bear fruit he prunes[a] so that it
> will be even more fruitful.*
> John 15:2

There are many things that will eventually become a
thorn in our flesh later if God does not take them from our
lives. God knows what things to be taken from us and what
He needs to put back.

Pruning is always a painful period since it is time when
God will take some of the things that you rely on to get
happiness. There is always a tendency of human nature to
let certain things go in our lives. Sometimes God requires
us to let everything go from our hands and start again.

> *Many are the plans in a person's heart, but it is the LORD's
> purpose that prevails.*
> Proverbs 19:21

The issue with many people today is that, they hear a
'word' from God and then set themselves off without waiting
on God for adequate preparation. Many people are tired,
confused and stuck on the path today in fulfilling their divine

destiny because they have run ahead of God's timing. When you run ahead of God, there is a potential of missing the efficacy or misunderstanding the message God gave you (2 Samuel 18: 19-33).

There are people who have the understanding of the dream God has given them but do not know what to do. An example was the great hero Moses. He knew that God had called him to deliver the children of Israel from bondage under Egyptians but Moses failed to understand God's plan and timing concerning Israel as it was declared to Abraham (Genesis 15:13). In your determination and willingness to accomplish your great dreams, it is vital you understand God's plan and timing for your life.

> *Moses thought that his own people would realize that God was using him to rescue them, but they did not.*
> Acts 7:25

Moses thought that killing the Egyptian was the way the Jews would recognise him as the person appointed by God to deliver the Israelites from slavery. In Exodus 12:40-41, the Bible says, 'now the length of time the Israelite people lived in Egypt[a] was 430 years.' 41 At the end of the 430 years, to the very day, all the LORD's divisions left Egypt. This indicates there was thirty years difference. It was revealed in the book of Acts that the 390th year was when Moses killed the Egyptian and fled from Egypt. Moses spent forty years on the desert and the difference between forty years and thirty years is ten years.

According to the Bible, Moses was ten years premature in trying to accomplish his divine calling. If Moses had understood God's timing and waited, he could have used only ten years in preparation for his job. Most people have become stagnant and impotent in delivering what God has deposited in them. Because they have run ahead of God's

89

timing. Education teaches man that we cannot jump from A to Z so as in our walk with God. Anytime we run ahead of God's timing, we have to pay the consequences. Moses paid the price for his action and the whole Israel had to wait because of him.

THE KEY TO WAITING FOR GOD'S PERFECT TIME IS NOT THE LENGTH OF TIME, BUT HOW WE HANDLE THE CHALLENGES WHILST WAITING.

When a person is deeply rooted in the word of God, he understands that timing is often the secret to attaining divine success. The Bible states, 'He has made everything beautiful in his own time' (Ecclesiastes 3:11).

Have you noticed something very strange in life? Two products will emerge into the market the same time, one will be better than the other one and yet fail. Why?

This is all because of wrong timing. One amazing thing in the Bible is that, the son of God (Jesus) was aware of his father's timing while he was on earth (John 7:6). Jesus used thirty years to prepare for a three-year mission on earth. In life, most people want to reap easily. There will be no reaping unless there is planting. God's timing has great influence in the life of everyone who wants to fulfil their divine destiny.

Many marriages are broken and ended in pain because of marrying at the wrong time. As far as God shows you who to marry does not necessary mean that you can marry on the spot. Preparation is very important in all areas of our lives if we want to see the hand of God move in our lives.

Some of the wise will stumble, so that they may be refined, purified and made spotless until the time of the end, for it will still come at the appointed time.
Daniel 11:35

God only operates within the confines and boundaries of his salvation principle. God requires us to wait for His appointed time regardless of the perceived gravity of our pains and physical needs. He causes us to wait in order for us to grow spiritually and mature in our walk with Him. He knows all the challenges we face but He is never late or never early to redeem us from falling. He is always on time.

Understanding God's timing is very vital and yet impossible without spiritual guidance from the word of God. The Bible gives an account of some great heroes and how long it took them to fulfil their God-given purpose. It took our father Abraham 27 years to be ready, 13 years for Joseph to be a prime minister, 13 years for David to become a king and 7 more years for him to rule the whole nation and 14 years for Paul to prepare for his ministry and many more.

All great heroes of the Bible were people who patiently waited on God. The life of Joseph demonstrates a true character of a person who waited perfectly despite all the suffering of being sold as a slave to a foreign land by his own family and all the challenges he had to overcome.

God operates with timing and for anyone to accomplish his or her God-given dream, it is important to recognize, understand and respond to God's timing.

PRINCIPLE 13

SELF-CONTROL

Webster defines self-control as 'control of one's feelings, desires or actions by one's own will; the power of controlling one's external reactions, emotions, etc.; equanimity.'

Lack of self-control has wrecked many people of their great dreams and goals in life because they failed to acknowledge the consequence it can have on them. A person's emotion, intellect and will must be under the subjection of the Holy Spirit. Without these three faculties of human personalities under the total control of the Holy Spirit, it is impossible for one to live a spiritual life and to possess mastery over his life.

We live in a world where self-control has lost its value in society but yet remains one of the greatest fundamental principles to attaining divine success. Long term achievement is determined by the persistent denials of our fleshy desires, which results in a true spiritual walk (Luke 9:25). Every dream a man desires to accomplish requires him to denial himself of certain things which can destroy his purpose and must bring himself under the authority of the Holy Spirit.

WHEN THERE IS LACK OF SELF-CONTROL, BIG DREAMS AND GOALS CAN CEASE TO MATERIALIZE.

Dreaming big is not enough but able to dream and also bring to pass. Many dreamers have abandoned their dreams due to their inability to control certain things in their life.

A report by Joni Meenagh stated that 'teenagers are going to have sex, nobody can stop this from happening.' (SIECUS Report, Apr/May 2003). This suggested that teenagers of today cannot have full control over the things they desire.

Joseph was a young man who demonstrated a valiant self-control. People who realise they are the purpose of God, live a life driven by God's guidance. Joseph was sold into slavery at the age of seventeen but mastered self-control regardless to all the numerous trials and temptations he faced. Many are those who would have lost focus and abandon their dreams. Joseph's dream was precious to him. This inspired him to endure in the mist of challenges. He valued his dream more than anything. The Bible states that, Joseph prospered in Potiphar's house because God was with him (Genesis 39:2). As he gained recognition, all eyes began to focus on him, especially his master's wife. Joseph was a loyal man who has gained the trust of his master. The Bible makes us know that, Joseph faced a bigger challenge when Potiphar's wife threw herself at him. However, instead of giving into the malice or wrong affair, he decided to run away.

WE MUST KNOW THAT THERE IS ALWAYS A BIGGER PURPOSE BEHIND OUR DIFFICULT SITUATIONS WHEN WE STAY FOCUS.

God's divine purpose is always greater than our problems. Obstacles are the things we see when we take our eyes from our dreams and goals. Joseph refused over and over again, until one day he left his cloak in her hands and ran out of the house. Potiphar's wife accused Joseph of raping her. Potiphar believed his wife and Joseph was taken to prison. Joseph without any lawyer to rescue him relied on God for protection.

Through all the temptations Joseph faced, he kept his relationship with God and denied his desires of the flesh. The faithfulness of Joseph caused God to grant him favour in the eyes of the prison warden. God had been silence in his life for a long time but he understood God was still preparing him whilst in prison.

DO NOT ALLOW YOUR CURRENT CIRCUMSTANCES TO DEFINE YOUR POSITION IN THE KINGDOM OF GOD.

Facing temptation is never easy. Potiphar's wife constantly tempted Joseph. Unlike Joseph, many youths would have given into the wickedness of Potiphar's wife. With great drive and willingness, we can learn to become like Joseph.

Ask God for strength concerning every weakness in your life in order to bring your dream to fulfillment.

Another report also shows that, the incredulity of youth today possessing self-control is very fashionable, even among the highly educated. For example, Richard Kneeling M.D said, "Teenagers are going to drink no matter what the legal age." (Milwaukee journal sentinel, 07/15/05).

In Daniel 1:1-21, four Hebrew men also demonstrated an astonishing character of self- control or mastery over themselves. Daniel, Meshak, Shadrack and Abednego were under training in Babylonia under the rule of Nebuchadnezzar. One facet of their training involves eating the food provided from the king's table. The Jews recognized food from the king's table as unclean according to their custom.

The four Hebrew men ate vegetables and water instead of the royal food. (Daniel 1:11-15). They could have chosen to drink like everyone else but chose to abstain from it because it was against God.

CONQUERING YOURSELF IS THE GREATEST CONQUEST.

The story of Sampson is one of the most pathetic stories in the Bible even though it carries strong significance. Samson was a man set apart by God to deliver the children of Israel from the oppression of Philistines (Judges 13:5). He was given a specific ordinance as how to live his life but chose his own path because of lack of self-control.

Samson was the strongest man yet weak. He could not control his sexual desire. Delilah presented him with a fine gift but Samson did not know that Delilah was the one his enemy were using to discover his strength. Through disobedience Samson took the opportunity and that lead him to his downfall. Not every woman is ordained by God to be in your life. Samson was able to accomplish his purpose through his death by asking God for mercy and strength. However his life still remains as a life of tragedy in history for lack of self-control.

There is no one in history who exhibited the character of self-control more than Jesus. His spirit lives in the inside of you once you believe in him. He was a spirit but came to this earth as a man. He showed the power of self-control. God has deposited something greater in you to accomplish and do not finish with pains and memories like Sampson. When lack of self-control is not carefully restrained, it can destroy your goals and dreams in life. You have the power to overcome self-control if only you will allow God to rule your life.

PRINCIPLE 14

GODLY CHARACTER

Oxford dictionary defines character as the mental and moral qualities distinctive to an individual.

Everyone possesses a character which can be considered either good or bad. Character here is not just a merely character but the building of a Godly Character. Godly Character is not genetic or possess through education or environment. It must be developed. Godly Character surpasses gender, race, education, religion, age and personality. Attaining a Godly Character begins with a relationship with God.

YOUR RELATIONSHIP WITH GOD IS WHAT GIVES BIRTH TO GODLY CHARACTER.

Godly Character can be defined as "the ability to discern God's right way from wrong and to voluntarily surrender one's own will to do what is right in God's sight and with the promised supernatural help, to resist the wrong even under pressure and temptation.

Your character is the oxygen of your divine destiny. As you need oxygen to survive, so as you need character to sustain the gift God has given you. No matter your charisma, if you lack Godly Character, you will crash. The anointing of God upon a man does two things; either makes you or breaks you, that it promotes or demote you of your glory. Many men with great destinies have been crashed, for lack of Godly Character.

There is a saying that the true beauty of a woman is not in her garments or her physical appearance so as character is not determined just by the outward appearance. Character is significantly a substance of the inside which reflects on the outside.

PEOPLE CAN FORGET YOUR ACHIEVEMENTS IN LIFE BUT CAN NEVER FORGET WHAT YOU ARE MADE OF.

Godly Character develops over time. A person's character is not formed early in life. Godly Character takes time to grow and it does not change easily. Joseph stood before Pharaoh at the age of thirty but was sold as a slave at the age of seventeen. His thirteen years was literally spent in valleys (pits). But it was the valley that prepared and proved his character. Difficulties and challenges are part of life. They are all necessary to achieve or attain Godly Character. Godly Character is only attained through the experience of adversities. Joseph overcame difficult times in order for Godly Character to be produced in his life.

> *And not only that, but we also glory in tribulations, knowing that tribulation produces perseverance; and perseverance, character; and character, hope. Now hope does not disappoint, because the love of God has been poured out in our hearts by the Holy Spirit who was given to us*
>
> Romans 5:3-5

Godly Character has great impact in the world we live today. The only long lasting solution to the problems the world is facing today such as gang activity, drug, racial

97

tensions, domestic violence, crime, alcohol abuse, broken homes school drop outs and many more can be only resolve through developing to improve our Godly Character.

Godly Character growth is vital to the fragmentary success of our society. The root cause of these problems is a result of lack of Godly Character in our societies. The society needs role models who have attained Godly Characters to affect the lives of other people.

As we examine the life of Joseph, we can say that he was a man of Godly Character. It is vital to know Joseph develop a Godly Character and what are the elements that formed Joseph's Godly Character.

Three aspect of Godly Character comprises of:

• INTEGRITY

Webster dictionary defines integrity as 'a firm adherence to a code of moral values'. Joseph was a man of integrity. One features of a Godly Character is integrity.

> The integrity of the upright guides them, but the unfaithful are destroyed by their duplicity.
>
> Proverbs 11:3

We live in a time where integrity has lost its power and means nothing to societies. Integrity does not mean perfection but a man of integrity is able to admit mistakes and repents from it.

Joseph's life shows a man who walked in integrity. He did not compromise the standard or the statutes of God. There are times when personal integrity will be tested to make certain decisions but integrity does what God says and does what is right even when no one is watching.

A man of integrity focuses on the future. Joseph saw beyond that the plan of God concerning the Israelites was not to live in Egypt but to move to Canaan.

• CREATIVITY

Godly Character displays an aspect of creativity. A person of creative wisdom is able to approach a need, a task or an idea from a different perspective. Joseph used his gift of interpreting dream to solve the economy of Egypt.

Many Christians have not come to understand their true identity and therefore loose sense of their power of creativity. Other men such as Daniel and Nehemiah also solved many issues during their time.

May God cause the world to search for you when they are looking for solutions in the name of Jesus. Everyone possesses the gift of creativity because we are created in the image of God (Genesis 1:27). God expects us to do great things because we are His workmanship (Ephesians 2:10).

> *"Everyone has the power for greatness - not for fame but greatness, because greatness is determined by service".*
>
> Dr Martin Luther King Jr

• EXCELLENCE

Excellence is another aspect of Godly Character. True success derives from being excellent at what you do. The biblical understanding of excellence is exercising completely your full potentials to bring glory to God.

An excellent Godly Character is a character that has been tested and approved and can stand against every storm and challenge of life. Character is not a destination but a journey.

An excellent character seeks to bear more fruits. It is always seeking to do greater things for God. An excellent filled man bears the fruit of the spirit (Galatians 5:22-23). Joseph was just a man like us yet he exhibited the fruit of the spirit. Your divine calling will give you a positive attitude towards achieving excellence.

THE UNDEVIATING AFFILIATION BETWEEN GODLY CHARACTER AND ACCOMPLISHMENT IS THAT YOU CANNOT HAVE ONE AND WITHOUT THE OTHER.

It is believed that character is the foundation for all true success. Although a person may have everything requisite for a good living such as money, position, or power, if he is unable to exhibit a "Godly Character he or she is not considered to be truly successful.

PRINCIPLE 15

TRUSTING GOD

Trust in the LORD with all your heartand lean not on your own understanding;in all your ways submit to him,and he will make your paths straight.

Proverbs 3:5-6

Trusting God means to have complete faith in Him and His word. Trusting God is not easy when all the negatives are stacked against you in life and everything seems to be falling apart.

Most of the time, when we encounter setbacks in life, we find it easy to trust in human devices rather than God. Regardless of how human knowledge has increased in recent years, it is however vital to know that human proficiency is limited. Trusting in God demonstrates an attitude of humility in God. It makes us know that man's intellectual knowledge is dependent on God. The Bible says 'cursed be anyone who trusts in man'.

Have you boarded an airplane before? Most of us do not even know the pilot but we enter the plane with hope that we will get to our destinations safely. When the plane you are flying on encounters some unexpected turbulence you do not tell the Air Hostess to open the door to get out, you sit still and trust the pilot.

Now let me ask you this question, do you trust God to take you from where you are right now into His perfect will concerning your life? If you answer 'YES', then you trust God to be the pilot of your destiny.

Joseph is one of the greatest heroes of the Bible whose authentic faith led him to accomplish his divine purpose on earth. What distinguishes him from others was his complete trust in God. He knew his strength came from God and for him to win every battle in life, he had to rely on God. Now what is faith?

Now faith is the substance of things hoped for, the evidence of things not seen.

Hebrew 11:1

The platform of God's kingdom is based on faith. Without faith it is impossible to please God (Hebrew 11:6). The word faith signifies both substance and evidence. Meaning there is an assurance and proof. So faith is also having confident assurance and confirmation of the promises we hope for but not seen.

Trusting God is moving from unrealities of hope and bringing them into the realm of reality by acting on God's word. Faith is your ticket to receiving every promise God has deposited with you. Your ticket is what gives you the right to access God's resources in His kingdom.

God released His word into Joseph's spirit. He held onto the word and kept the word in his heart. Joseph just believed in the word and was expectant of his dream even when he had not yet seen it. Faith transcends beyond the five senses of man. It is a heavenly material of what you desire in your heart.

FAITH IS ALSO A SUPERNATURAL POWER THAT RULES OVER NATURE AND ALSO ENABLES MAN TO ACCOMPLISH THEIR DIVINE PURPOSE OF GOD ON EARTH.

God has placed a word in everyone's spirit but until faith is applied, it is just a word. Faith is what produces the result we need. The Bible says, 'the just shall live by faith' (Habakkuk 2:4).

Just as we constantly breathe in oxygen so should we faith. You live with it, move with it and sleep with it and all other things depend on your faith in God. Fasting and prayer does not change God. Faith changes things. Faith always says it is mine. Mark 11:24 teaches us to believe and receive.

- Faith is the word.
- Believing is acting on the word.
- Believing and acting is what causes things to give birth.

Faith without works is dead so as words without action is dead (James 2:17-19).

Faith is not complete without obedience. When we believe (trust) God with all our heart, we will obey (keep) His commandments. Walking by faith is not easy when everything seems wrong and all the odds are stacked against you. Joseph could have been the first to conceive doubts but he kept his eyes on the promises of God.

Faith does not exempt us from trouble. The Bible declares in John 16:13 that we will have troubles in this world. As long as we live on this planet, we have to fight everyday but fight the good fight of faith (1 Timothy 6:12). Faith does not make things easy but makes all things possible.

THE WORD OF GOD HAS AUTHORITY TO TRANSFORM LIVES BUT UNTIL FAITH IS APPLIED, IT BECOMES DESTITUTE OF ITS POWER.

The life of Joseph shows a man who had an intimacy

with God so as all the heroes of the Bible. Many people do not have faith in God because they do not have any relationship with Him. Your relationship with God determines how much you know him. Knowing God is the first step for everyone who truly wants to enjoy his blessings. Faith develops when we establish a deeper relationship with God.

Having Faith in God will enable you to:

• Acquire Godly Wisdom

Wisdom is the ability to apply God's word effectively. When you fear God, he gives you wisdom which enables you to discern what is wrong and right in His sight. The fear of God is the beginning of wisdom (Proverb 9:10). The fear of the Lord is to hate evil and every step of Joseph proved a man who feared God (Proverb 8:13). Joseph walked upright with God and God gave him wisdom (Proverb 2:7).

Pharaoh noticed the wisdom of Joseph was not from the world but from the spirit of the Lord (Genesis 41:39). Pharaoh could not compare the wisdom of Joseph to any of his magicians or anyone in Egypt.

Joseph's wisdom helped him to give thought to all his ways (Proverbs 14:8). He was of understanding and used the wisdom of God to govern his life. Anyone who yearns for God's blessing and prosperity needs wisdom.

> *For wisdom is protection just as money is protection, but the advantage of knowledge is that wisdom preserves the lives of its possessors".*

Ecclesiastes 7:12

• Experience His Power

When we operate by faith; we rest in the divine authority of God to release His strength to work on our behalves.

Joseph relied on God for both his spiritual and physical needs. For Joseph to overcome all the plans of the enemy concerning his life, he had to depend totally on God. He knew his source of strength was from God. The Bible says, 'a branch cannot bear fruit without the vine (John 15:4).'

Many Christians are frustrated because of their inability to abide in God. Pharaoh was a pagan king who did not trust in the God of Abraham, Isaac and Jacob but did plainly admit the power of God which was at work in Joseph's life (Genesis 39:3). God's power becomes active in you when you dwell under the authority of His word (Psalm 91:1). Joseph did greater Exploits through the power of God (Daniel 11:32).

• Experience His Peace

The peace of God offers the assurance that regardless of what happens you know it is well with your soul. Joseph's heart was not troubled. God says, My peace I give you. I do not give to you as the world gives. Do not let your hearts be troubled and do not be afraid." (John 14:27)

The peace of God comes from knowing him. Joseph learned to stand still and was anxious of nothing believing God will bring everything to pass. He knew God's peace surpasses all understanding (Philippians 4:6-7).

The peace of God brings an inner tranquillity and stability in the mist of all difficult circumstances. The Bible says, 'If God be for us who can be against us' (Romans 8:31).

Joseph, a man with a big dream, found himself in a pit. He could have doubted God's promises concerning his life. Most of us would have thrown in the towel. Joseph might not have understood what he was going through yet trusted God with all his heart. Joseph's trust in God did not go unnoticed by God. God designed a plan that will bring Joseph from prison. This is what Joseph had been waiting for all his years of misery.

THE DEFINING MOMENT OF HIS LIFE

God was still working on Joseph whiles in prison. Joseph had been waiting for just one moment of his life that could bring him total freedom and to catapult him to his dream fulfilment. God had a master plan for him.

> But the eyes of the LORD are on those who fear him, on those whose hope is in his unfailing love.
>
> Psalm 33:18

Joseph had passed every test and it was time for God to change the identity of his suffering servant and restore him to his leadership position. Joseph earned God's trust by walking with Him.

Can God trust you in a position of responsibility?

God knew Joseph could handle his leadership position now without bringing any disgrace to him.

In Genesis 41:1-36, the Bible records that King Pharaoh had a dream but none of his magicians and wise men could interpret them.

> Pharaoh said to Joseph, "I had a dream, and no one can interpret it. But I have heard it said of you that when you hear a dream you can interpret it."
>
> Genesis 41:15

Joseph did not only interpret Pharaoh's dream but also gave plans to deal with the coming years of famine (Genesis 41:36-45). The Bible says, 'King's heart is in His hands of the Lord' (Proverbs 21:1). Pharaoh recognised the interpretation made sense and it was good in his eyes and all his servants. Pharaoh realised the spirit of God was at work in Joseph's life and there was no one as wise as him. Pharaoh knew God was with Joseph and everything was revealed to him. Pharaoh appointed Joseph to become his second in command (Prime Minister). Joseph was exalted over all the people of Egypt. Pharaoh declared to Joseph his position and authority that could not be denied by any one in Egypt. Joseph had been forgotten and left in prison, but he was just a second from his exaltation.

Genesis 41:42-57, the Bible records that Pharaoh took off his signet ring from his finger and put it on Joseph's finger, dressed him in robes of fine linen and put a gold chain around his neck as a symbol of restoration of honour, glory and full authority. Joseph was displayed in Pharaoh's second chariot before all the people to be publically accepted as Pharaoh's second in command. Pharaoh also declared unto Joseph, without him no man can lift his hand or foot in the land of Egypt. Joseph was given Pharaoh's full protection and approval to lead the nation. This was a position of great honour of power bestowed upon Joseph.

God continued to bless Joseph in the province of Egypt and he forgot all his misery and continued to be fruitful because God was with him (Genesis 39:2).

The Bible says, 'the blessing of the LORD, it makes rich, and he adds no sorrow with it' (Proverbs 10:22).

The fulfilment of Joseph's dream also confirmed the promise God declared to Abraham concerning the children of Israel (Genesis 15:13-16). His dream was not only about him but a dream which unlocked the destiny of many generations. Joseph was not only blessed but through the famine, God reconciled him to his family. He told his brothers not to be afraid and forgave their wrong deeds and explained to them why God had sent him to Egypt though they meant evil for him (Genesis 50:20-21). The man who was hated, conspired to kill, abused, accused, and imprisoned, forgotten has become channel of blessings to many nations. The Bible says, 'The stone which the builders rejected has become the head stone of the corner' (Psalm 118:22, Acts 4:11).

Joseph's life story is not only evidence of faith and confidence during years of sorrow and tragedy, but also a story full of joy, peace, prosperity and success. God does not lie and His word will always prevail. Joseph did not die and no one believed in his dream but it finally came to reality.

God is not a man, that he should lie, nor a son of man, that he should change his mind. Does he speak and then not act? Does he promise and not fulfil?

Numbers 23:19

CONCLUSION

Yet, O LORD, you are our Father. We are the clay, you are the potter; we are all the work of your hand"
Isaiah 64:8

The potter has completed His work. Every earthen vessel God wants to use for a greater manifestation has to go through a process of moulding. There is a treasure in every earthen vessel (2 Corinthians 4:7).

Through thirteen years of trials, Joseph was trained, shaped and fully equipped for his leadership position.

God is our creator and He has the authority to mould us according to His perfect will. Joseph might not have fully understood the significance of his suffering from the beginning but realised none was wasted at the end. God was with him throughout his suffering.

During his time of slavery and imprisonment, he learned the language and tradition of Egyptians which he needed in the future. In prison, he learned that servanthood is an important key to divine leadership. He understood that a position of authority is a place of service to mankind and not fame. He also met the chief butler who later became his destiny helper by recommending him to King Pharaoh through the grace of God.

God wants all his faithful children to learn and show themselves approved in everything. Joseph also understood one vital element of leadership is stewardship. Everyone will give an account to God for what he has been entrusted with (Romans 14:12). Also he established a strong foundation for his leadership position.

Joseph also learned one of the most astonishing and vital truths many do not recognise today. He came to a much deeper and fuller knowledge of God's sovereignty when he was put in position. He realised it is God's grace and favour that brought him triumph. He understood why God used his adversity to set him up for such a blessing. Knowing this brought him much deeper understanding of humility. He gave all the glory to God and did not take pride in anything. He lived in Egypt with all his family till his death.

Joseph's life was marked by deeper awareness of God. His story depicts a man who trusted and walked closely with God throughout his life. Joseph found true meaning and purpose in his life.

Our challenges and difficulties can make us do unpleasant things. You may be going through a time of sorrow, a broken relationship, facing financial disaster, sickness, death of a loved one, or feel you have failed in life. Do not consider your current circumstances to determine your future. Trust in God with all your heart and he will mould you better and lift you higher and higher. He holds the final blueprint of your destiny. The Bible says, 'He raises the poor from the dust and lifts the needy from the ash heap; he seats them with princes' (1 Samuel 2:8).

No matter how insignificant our lives may seem to be, God still has a better plan for us. The Psalmist said, "But the plans of the LORD stand firm forever, the purposes of his heart through all generations" (Psalm 33:11).

God has special ways to use every blood bought and sanctified by His Amazing Grace to bring glory and honour to His name. In every fruit lies a seed and every seed has the ability to be become a forest. Do not count yourself out.

I believe you have been blessed through reading this book. I pray that you will apply these wisdom principles to overcome every limitation and take charge of your life and fulfil your dreams. You are a winner already as you take the first step towards your dream.

Remember, you are destined to achieve and No weapon formed against you shall prosper (Isaiah 54:17).

I waited patiently for the LORD; he turned to me and heard my cry. He lifted me out of the slimy pit, out of the mud and mire; he set my feet on a rock and gave me a firm place to stand. He put a new song in my mouth, a hymn of praise to our God. Many will see and fear and put their trust in the LORD. Blessed is the man who makes the LORD his trust, who does not look to the proud, to those who turn aside to false gods. Many, O LORD my God, are the wonders you have done. The things you planned for us no one can recount to you; were I to speak and tell of them, they would be too many to declare (Psalm 40:1-5).

GOD RICHLY BLESS YOU!

*If you were blessed by reading this wonderful book
and want to give any extra comments,
order some more copies, or want to contact the author,
please use the contact details below:*

Email: boantwi@gmail.com
Website: www.boapublishers.com
Website: www.bernardoaantwi.com
facebook: Bernard O A Antwi
Mobile: (0044) 7830516916

Notes

Notes

Notes